Sandwich Exotica
The Sandwich Manual for Connoisseurs

by
LOUIS P. De GOUY

Running Press, Philadelphia

Copyright © 1975 Running Press
All Rights Reserved Under the Pan-American and International Copyright Conventions
Printed in the United States of America

Distributed in Canada by Van Nostrand Reinhold, Ltd., Ontario

ISBN 0-914 294-39-3 (Paperback Edition)
ISBN 0-914 294-40-7 (Library Edition)

Book Concept: Diane Denbo Stevens
Art Direction: Jim Wilson
Cover Art: Todd Schorr

This book may be ordered directly from the publisher. Please include 25¢ postage.
Try your bookstore first.

Running Press, 38 South 19th Street, Philadelphia, Pennsylvania 19103

This book was discovered by Diane Denbo Stevens behind a dusty stack of books in an antique shop near New Hope, Pennsylvania.

In 1939 **Sandwich Exotica** made its first appearance under the title **Sandwich Manual for Professionals**. From the original title and succinct presentations of sandwich ingredients it becomes obvious that the book was intended for professional restaurateurs and chefs as an aid in designing menus.

We believe that everyone in their own way is a sandwich professional. **Sandwich Exotica** is just a tool for stretching your imagination.

At the end of **Sandwich Exotica** you will find an exceptionally complete and very handy alphabetically arranged index. If you look a little further you will discover a *Sandwich Cost Table For Professionals*. The tables were compiled in the late 30's and are not intended for today's use. They are so hopelessly out of date that we felt you would find them humorous and sad at the same time.

SANDWICHES

3   ORIGIN OF SANDWICHES

The Greeks and the Romans enjoyed a wedge of meat between two slabs of bread, and so did the Babylonians, without a doubt, but it was the fourth Earl of Sandwich that made the English people sandwich minded and give the world a habit-forming luncheon—and it was the noble use to which the eighteenth century playboy ever put his noble name. However, it was the invention of the great Jewish teacher, Rabbi Hillel, the prince who lived between 70 B.C. and 70 A.D.

The Jewish people during the Passover feast ritual still follow Hillel's custom of eating sandwich made of two pieces of matzoh (unleavened bread) containing mohror (bitter herbs) and haroseth (chopped nuts and apple, to resemble the mortar of the Egyptians) as a reminder of Hebrew suffering before the Deliverance from Egypt. This is to prove that sandwiches are as old as bread and cheese, and Romans and Danes and Saxons and Normans must have eaten them from one end of England to the other.

Sandwiches today, are (or ought to be) real food, served in a convenient form where knives and forks are out of place, except for certain ones, and above all, made of such—a functional food, if there ever was one. Even a tea sandwich should set out to be good before it aims to be dainty, for if a patron calls for honest bits of nourishment (sometimes very small bits) and not just multicolored slivers tortured into strange shapes, or plastered together with synthetic spreads for folks who counts calories or wish to keep slim. Remember, that sandwiches, which are in existence to assuage the pangs of hunger should not be made paper-thin and completely tasteless. Sandwiches are not canapés, and canapés are not sandwiches, although the very same spread may be used for both.

4 Do's and Don'ts in Making Sandwiches

Traditionally day-old bread is supposed to be used, because it's easier to cut, but if you have a sharp knife and keep it horizontal as you cut with a sawing motion even fresh bread (and many a patron calls for fresh bread nowadays) may be cut easily into thick or thin slices. The slicing of bread should be done ahead of time. Then comes the spread or spreads which may be plain butter, creamed butter (see "Creamed Butters No. 149 up to No. 167 included") or one of the spreads indicated for canapés (Recipe No. 65, "Canapé Spread Suggestions" up to No. 97 included), or one of your own creation or imagination. These spreads should be soft enough to be spread thinly and evenly with a knife blade, or a wooden or bone spatula.

In placing meat or meats on spread, be sure all four corners are covered. This means a proper distribution of the filling in the sandwich, so that the patron biting near the edge will find something besides bread. The spread or meat, or fish, or whatever be the filling, may be covered with clean, crisp lettuce leaves, cabbage (red or green) watercress, cole slaw, or other greens. These greens as well as the filling should not protrude over the sides of the bread, but should be neatly trimmed with or without the crust.

To raise ready sandwich from the board to the plate, always use sandwich knife or spatula and the tips of fingers. Never pick the sandwich from the board with your hand and do not slide it from the board onto a sandwich plate, which by the way should be hot, for hot sandwich and cold for cold sandwich. Do not place a sandwich on a damp or wet plate. Sandwiches prepared in advance should be kept in a cool place, covered with a clean damp towel. However, never prepare salad or fruit or any dressed filling in advance, lest they become soggy and unfit to be served.

There are different kinds of sandwiches which may be served hot or cold, on plain bread, fancy bread, on toast or between sliced roll; open-faced, double or triple decked, pinwheel and the loaf or layer sandwich. The pinwheel and loaf or layer sandwich may be prepared in advance and sliced to order.

Under no circumstances do not use too stale a bread, unless requested by patron. Where toast is used for sandwich, butter the toast immediately it is done. This will keep it from drying too quickly, and preserves the moisture. Cold dry toast should never be used. Reserve it for croutons for soup or pudding; save also the bread and toast trimmings for the same purpose and for crumbing. Burned toast or scraped burned toast should never be used.

5 Sandwich Garnishings

The difference which garnishings make to a dish, be it a plain or an elaborate one is simply unbelievable until you see it with your own eyes. Garnishing, decorating and trimming are to the decorative ensemble of a dish what accessories are to a dress ensemble. And, like dress accessories, they should be chosen with taste, with a sure sense of their appropriateness. The shape, color and edible texture of these accessories should always be suitable to the dish on which they are used, and should harmonize with the decorative scheme of the dish, exactly as are the make-ups of a woman.

Garnishing dishes is today more imperative than ever before on account of keen competition, and also because a customer is a mighty exacting individual. He not only expects good food, but he demands it and must have it.

There are so many plain, neat and inexpensive garnishings that their listing here will require many pages. Here are a few suggestions:

Apples—Cubed, sliced, in ring, rolled in paprika, minced parsley, chives or curry powder.

Cheese—Cubed, sliced, rolled into small balls, then in paprika, parsley, curry powder, saffron, nuts, chives, etc.

Dill Pickles—Cubed, sliced, cut fan-like, in sticks or in cups and filled with cottage cheese or mayonnaise.

Green Pepper—In cups, sliced in rings, chopped.

Hard-Cooked Eggs — Chopped, sliced, quartered, halved, sieved, then mixed with minced parsley, chives, chopped dill, or capers.

Horseradish—Plain or mixed with prepared mustard or dressing, fresh and shredded, in small balls, mixed with cottage cheese, etc.

Lemon—Sliced thin, dipped in paprika or minced parsley or chives or in cups, filled with dressing, etc.

Lettuce—Shredded, crisp leaves, in cups, then filled with dressing.

Mint—Especially for lamb sandwiches; fresh mint leaves, mint jelly cubes, etc., or mint jelly, chopped.

Olives—Black, green, ripe or stuffed, scooped, filled with cottage cheese or horseradish, etc.

Parsley—Which should be crisp and fresh, minced, sprig or bunches.

Pimiento—Sliced, chopped, in cups, etc., filled with minced onion, etc.

Radishes — Sliced, dressed with mayonnaise, or scooped and filled with horseradish, mayonnaise or cheese.

Relishes—As tomato and onion; pickled beets, spiced string beans, curried tomato relish, chow-chow, pickled cucumbers and onion slices, cabbage relish, cole slaw, red or green, pickled cauliflowers, etc.

Tomatoes—Ripe or green, sliced, quartered, halved then filled with almost anything which is edible, as chopped nuts, creamed cheese with nuts, or olives, or fruit, etc.

Watercress—Which should be crisp and green, using either sprigs or a generous bunch.

All of these left to the innate taste or talent, or imagination of the sandwich maker.

HOT SANDWICH SUGGESTIONS

Unless otherwise indicated, all recipes are for 1 person.

6   Bacon and Tomato Sandwich

Broil 3 slices of bacon and put between slices of toast with crisp lettuce and sliced tomato, the latter raw or broiled with the bacon.

7   Baked Beans Cheesewitch

On a slice of bread, toasted on both sides, spread with heated baked beans (canned or otherwise). Top with thin slice of American cheese; place under broiler until cheese melts. Cover with 2 broiled strips of bacon; then with crisp lettuce, and top with a piece of toast.

8   Baked Beans Rarebit Sandwich

Grate or run through food chopper some American cheese. Add enough melted butter to make a soft enough spreading mixture. Spread thickly on slices of bread. Mash some baked beans (canned), heat and season to taste with salt, pepper, a little prepared mustard or catsup, and a scant teaspoon grated onion. Put two slices of bread together, cheese side in, with a filling of bean mixture between. Toast or brown in butter in a frying pan. Serve at once.

9   Boiled Beef Sandwich

Place a slice of bread on the centre of a hot plate; cover with a slice of hot boiled beef; spread with prepared horseradish. You may serve a scoop of mashed potatoes and one of buttered peas.

10   Broiled Ham Sandwich

Place a thin slice of broiled ham between two thin slices of bread, having or not crisp lettuce between the ham. Serve with a scoop of mashed potatoes, a pickle and a slice of ripe tomato.

11   Broiled Tomato Sandwich

Wash a ripe tomato, slice thick, season with salt and pepper to taste and dip in oil or bacon fat. Broil on both sides and put between slices of buttered toast, previously covered with crisp lettuce leaves.

12   Cape Cod Sandwich

Two slices of buttered hot toast; a generous layer of creamed flaked crabmeat, not too moist, slice of American cheese, melted in the broiling oven; topped with the second piece of toast; served immediately, cut in quarters, garnished with a piece of dill pickle.

13   Chicken Sandwich

Slice chicken meat thin and keep hot on steam table. Serve the same as Roast Beef Sandwich, using a gravy made from chicken stock. Mashed potatoes and string beans may be served on the side.

14   Chicken Briarcliff Manor Sandwich

On a slice of freshly made toast, arrange slices of hot chicken and sugar-cured ham freshly broiled, a crisp lettuce leaf and a large slice of broiled tomato. Repeat the process after covering with a slice of toast. Flank the sandwich with strips of dill pickle, alternating with black olives. Serve hot with a scoop of peas, placed in a scooped, parboiled small green pepper, dusted with parsley.

15   Corned Beef Sandwich

Same as Boiled Beef No. 9. Serve hot horseradish sauce and boiled potato and a slice of dill pickle.

16   **Corned Beef Hash Sandwich**

Place a slice of plain bread, spread with prepared mustard on a hot plate and cover with Corned Beef Hash. Pour highly seasoned brown gravy over all. Serve with a few French fried potatoes.

17   **Creamed Tuna Sandwich**

Put slice of hot toast on hot plate. Spread with anchovy paste, and heap with creamed tuna fish. Top with lettuce leaves, then with another piece of toast, also spread with anchovy paste. Top the halved sandwich with a slice of broiled tomato.

Any kind of left-over cooked fish may be prepared this way.

18   **Cube Steak Sandwich**

Put a grilled cube steak (grilled one minute on each side) between two slices of toast spread with prepared mustard. Pour over highly seasoned brown sauce. Serve with a scoop of mashed potatoes and 1 scoop of creamed cabbage. Garnish with a dill pickle.

19   **Denver Sandwich**
                   (Serves 6)

Mix 1 lb. chopped—not ground—raw ham, 2 well-beaten raw eggs, 1 teaspoon onion juice and season to taste with salt and pepper. Heat 1 generous tablespoon bacon fat in a frying pan. Pour the mixture and cook over a low flame for 5 short minutes, stirring occasionally. Spread on slices of buttered toast, cover with another slice of toast and serve immediately, garnished with cole slaw.

20   **Fish Cake Sandwich**

Place 1 or 2 fried fish cakes between 2 slices of bread; cover with tomato sauce; garnish with French fried potatoes and a black olive.

21   Fried Chicken Sandwich

Meat may be cut away from the bone before or after frying. Serve the same as Roast Beef Sandwich No. 34. Garnish with French fried potatoes, and buttered peas.

22   Fried Egg Sandwich

Place a fried egg between 2 pieces of toast (the egg fried on both sides, the yolk broken and spread). Serve garnished with a slice of dill pickle placed over a lettuce leaf.

23   Fried Egg and Green Pepper Sandwich

Beat an egg slightly and add 1 tablespoon of chopped green pepper. Fry on both sides. Serve on toast or bread which has been spread with butter. Garnish with a scoop of mashed potatoes and a sprig of parsley.

24   Fried Egg and Onion Sandwich

Proceed as indicated for No. 23, Fried Egg and Green Pepper, substituting onion fried in butter until soft and mixed with the slightly beaten egg. Garnish with a slice of tomato.

25   Fried Egg and Tomato Sandwich

Same as Fried Egg and Green Pepper No. 23, substituting 1 tablespoon of stewed tomatoes for green pepper. Garnish with a black olive placed over a piece of lettuce leaf and topped with a slice of green pepper.

26   Fried Ham Sandwich

Ham may be fried in advance and kept hot on a steam table, but it will be tastier if served hot from the frying pan. Fry a thin slice of ham in the usual way, and place between two slices of toast spread with prepared mustard, each slice covered with lettuce leaves. Garnish with a scoop of mashed potatoes and 1 piece of dill pickle.

27   Ham and Egg Sandwich

Fry a slice of ham on one side; turn over and break an egg on top. When the egg begins to harden, turn the ham and egg over and cook the egg on the other side, breaking the yolk. Ham and egg sandwich may be kept hot on steam table between sheets of heavy wax paper. Garnish with a few French fried potatoes and an olive.

28   Ham and Swiss Cheese Sandwich

On one side of buttered bread, place a layer of Swiss cheese with mustard between 2 piece of freshly broiled ham. Place a second piece of buttered bread on top and toast on both sides. Cut diagonally and arrange a slice of tomato which has been broiled and seasoned to taste. Garnish with a stalk of crisp celery, placed on a piece of lettuce and a red radish.

29   Hamburger Sandwich

Place 1 or 2 steak patties on top of a slice of bread, or toast, or between a split roll, either spread with prepared mustard, and cover with brown gravy. Garnish with a few French fried and 1 scoop of buttered peas.

30   Lamb Sandwich

Operate as indicated for Boiled Beef Sandwich No. 9, substituting lamb for boiled beef, the bread spread with mustard butter. Garnish with creamed cabbage and a sprig of fresh mint.

31   Lamb Hash Sandwich

Same as Corned Beef Hash No. 16, substituting lamb hash for corned beef hash. Garnish with a few potato chips and a piece of dill pickle, placed on a lettuce leaf.

32   Liver and Bacon Sandwich

Fry 2 slices of bacon until crisp; drain off nearly all fat and fry a slice of beef liver in the remaining bacon fat (almost nothing). Put bacon, liver and a half hard-cooked egg through food chopper with a slice of onion and a tiny bit (optional) of garlic, ½ teaspoon of prepared horseradish and 1 teaspoon sour cream. Spread thickly on white bread or rye bread, buttered and with crusts removed. Cut in quarters; arrange each quarter on a piece of lettuce, and garnish center with potato chips. Garnish with a piece of gherkin and a sprig of watercress.

33   Pork Sandwich

Same as Lamb Sandwich No. 30. Garnish with a thick ring of apple fried in butter and browned on both sides, placing in center of the apple ring a large black olive, rolled in olive oil.

You may serve a scoop of mashed potatoes and a scoop of green vegetables, sprinkling the mashed potatoes with minced parsley.

34   Roast Beef Sandwich

Place a slice of bread, unbuttered on the centre of a hot plate; cover it with a slice of hot roast beef (about 3 to 3½ ounces). Cover with a rich brown gravy made from the stock of the roast. Sprinkle the gravy with green peas, and garnish with a strip of dill pickle and a scoop of mashed potatoes.

35   Salmon Club Sandwich

Drain canned salmon; remove skin and bones thoroughly and carefully. Leave salmon in large whole pieces. For each serving, arrange crisp lettuce leaves and salmon pieces, slightly heated on steam table on one slice of hot buttered toast. Top with 2 slices broiled bacon, and 1 slice of broiled tomato. Repeat the process after covering with a piece of toast, seasoning each layer to taste with salt and pepper. Top sandwich with slice of cucumber, seasoned to taste and garnish with scallions, radishes and dill pickle. Serve at once.

36   Sardine Club Sandwich

Cover a slice of buttered toast with a layer of sardines. Place slices of grilled tomatoes on the sardines, cover with lettuce leaves, and repeat the process, adding to the second layer, a few slices of cucumber or thin ring of onion, broiled brown under the flame of the broiling oven. Top with another slice of buttered bread and garnish with a scoop of creamed potatoes, sprinkled with minced pimientos.

37   Sardine and Egg Sandwich au Gratin

Spread toast with mashed sardines mixed with butter and a little prepared mustard. Sprinkle over the sardines, chopped hard-cooked egg then cover with medium white sauce and sprinkle generously with grated cheese. Brown under the flame of the broiling oven. Serve at once garnished with a dill pickle slice, an olive and a radish, placed over a lettuce leaf.

38   Scrambled Egg Sandwich

Spread an egg scrambled in the usual way, over a piece of toast spread with anchovy butter No. 454. Cover with 2 slices of crisp bacon; cut sandwich in quarters, and garnish center with a few French fried potatoes. Add a sprig or two of watercress. Serve at once.

39   Steak Sandwich

Steak may be fried sauteed or broiled. Serve dry, open-faced or with a rich brown gravy around, but not over the steak, with a few shoestring or French fried potatoes or onions. Garnish with several sprigs of crisp watercress.

40   Steak and Eggplant Sandwich

Steak may be broiled, fried or panned. Serve dry on a piece of bread. On another piece, open-faced-like sandwich, place a slice of fried eggplant, and surround with Spanish sauce. Garnish with a scoop of mashed potatoes, sprinkled with tiny fried croutons or fried breadcrumbs.

41   Steak and French Fried Onions Sandwich

Steak may be broiled, fried or panned. Serve dry or with a rich brown gravy. Place steak upon a slice of bread in centre of a hot plate. On another slice, arrange French fried onions. Garnish with a tablespoon each of buttered string beans and buttered carrots.

42   Steak and Fried Tomatoes Sandwich

Steak may be broiled, fried or panned. Serve dry or with a rich brown gravy. Place steak upon a piece of bread in centre of a hot plate. On another slice of bread, spread with garlic butter, arrange a large slice of fried tomato. Garnish with a scoop of mashed potatoes and a piece of dill pickle, placed upon a crisp lettuce leaf.

43   Tomato Buns Sandwich

Split round, flat, soft roll (buns) three-quarters open and spread generously with peanut butter, then with mayonnaise. Place in a large slice of broiled tomato and 2 slices of crisp hot bacon. Serve garnished with a scoop of buttered peas and 1 scoop of mashed potatoes. Garnish with sprigs of watercress and 1 large black olive.

44   Tongue Sandwich

Heat cold cooked tongue slices in meat or chicken broth, or in brown gravy. Place 2 or 3 slices upon a plain slice of bread; cover with a thick layer of spinach, and pour over hot egg sauce. Serve with a scoop of mashed potatoes and a slice of dill pickle.

45   Turkey Sandwich

Prepare and serve same as hot Chicken Sandwich, No. 13, substituting hot turkey slices for hot chicken slices.

46   Turkey and Mushroom Sauce Sandwich

Serve the same as Turkey Sandwich, above (No. 45). Pour over sizzling hot mushroom sauce.

47   Veal Cutlet Sandwich

Place a fried veal cutlet between two slices of bread or serve on top of bread with a brown gravy topping and a garnishing of French fried potatoes and a fried apple ring, placing in center of the ring a ripe olive or a red radish.

48   Wall Street Sandwich

Toast 2 slices of bread, cover one with sliced cheese, add a dash of cayenne and top with 2 half slices of raw bacon. Toast under a broiler until cheese melts and bacon is cooked. Butter the second slice of toast, top with lettuce and sliced tomatoes seasoned with salt and pepper. Arrange hot and cold open-faced sandwiches on plate; garnish with pickle relish in lettuce cup.

49   Welsh Rarebit Sandwich

Prepare an ordinary Welsh Rarebit. Serve on toast or plain bread. Garnish with olive and a stick of dill pickle.

50   Western Sandwich

Beat an egg slightly and add 1 tablespoon chopped cooked chicken and 1 tablespoon chopped pimiento. Fry in a small frying pan on both sides and serve on toast spread with horseradish butter. Garnish with a broiled tomato slice placed upon a crisp lettuce leaf, and 1 large black olive, stone removed, and substituted with cream cheese mixed with chopped walnut meats.

CHEESE SANDWICHES AND CHEESE COMBINATION FILLINGS

51   Cheese

Cheese is a profitable item to list on your menu, because cheese, like meat, is a rich, highly concentrated food, is one of the main reasons why there are so many demands for cheese sandwich. Another of the major reasons why cheese is favored by the American public is that cheese is not hard to digest as is often thought. However, it should be eaten with some other food—bread, for instance—so that the particles of cheese cannot pack together in the stomach.

The most used cheese in America is first the American cheese or Cheddar cheese, named for the quaint old village near the city of Bristol, England, but made on a grand scale in America. The type of American cheese easiest to use in the making of sandwiches is the oblong five pound loaf. It should be cut thinly on a meat or special slicer, or, if a hand knife is used, a piece of wax paper should be placed between each slice of cheese, to prevent sticking.

Next to American cheese, came Cream cheese, made in America, and which has no peer anywhere in the world. Right after Cream cheese came Swiss cheese, domestic or imported. The Wisconsin Swiss cheese industry grew so rapidly during these last few years that Southern Wisconsin became known as the "Switzerland of America." Most of it is made by Swiss-Americans—some of them born in sight of the Alps. Those eyes in Swiss cheese are what determine its grade and hence its price, for to a large extent they indicate the quality of the flavor. They should be neither too large nor too small, uniform in size and appearance and evenly distributed.

Whether you call it Schmier-Kase, Dutch Cheese, Clabber Cheese, Fromage à la Crème, or just plain Cottage Cheese or Pot Cheese, you will probably be serving this delectable and wholesome food in your place. The story of the cottage cheese is still a mystery, with its beginning hidden in the past, but it is assumed that this simply-made dairy product—and in great demand—came into being in small homes and cottages. And its name followed just as have other famous cheeses, from the town of their discovery or manufacture.

Cottage cheese blends so perfectly with various fruits and garnishes and adapts itself to so many different forms of serving in either hot or cold dishes, that the first thing necessary is to become acquainted with some of the many delicious—and inexpensive—dishes. Blended with sour cream and well-seasoned, it affords a delicious spread. Cottage cheese, or its counterpart, sweet cream cheese, is, of course, one of the most familiar standbys of the sandwich-maker. It may be made sweet with minced preserved fruits, dates, raisins, honey, and fruit juices, or, on the other hand, be transformed into a spicy devilled type of filling by combining with olives, anchovies, pickles, mustard, minced chives and parsley, watercress, etc. These mixtures may be packed into jars, and labelled, kept ready for emergency or rush. In many usual recipes calling for cheese, grated or cut fine, cottage cheese may often be substituted. Any type cottage cheese is a highly perishable product, and should be stored in the coolest place and disposed of as soon as possible.

Generous sized cheese sandwiches give skimpy menus full nourishment value as well as the needed quota of calcium, phosphorous and vitamin essentials.

Camembert, Roquefort and Liederkranz, have a special appeal with rye, brown and whole wheat bread as well as relishes. Cover all parts of the sandwich bread with the cheese when making sandwiches and serve with or without clean, crisp lettuce leaves. Put cheese through the food chopper when it is used in creamed or scalloped mixture, or when combined with other ingredients for a sandwich spread.

Overcooking of cheese results in a tough, leathery food, but the havoc does not stop there. Cheese contains more or less fat, and fat, as you know, decomposes when subjected to high heat.

52 American Cheese and Caviar Sandwich

Squeeze onion juice over buttered toast from which crusts have been trimmed. Spread with caviar. Over this pour a sauce made by melting butter and blending in a little flour until it forms a smooth paste; gradually add enough milk, stirring to prevent lumps; then stir in enough grated cheese and equal parts of mushroom, ground. Season to taste with salt and pepper, and pour over the caviar on toast. Dust with paprika. Serve hot.

53   American Cheese Sandwich

Cut the cheese thinly on a meat slicer, or, if a hand knife is used, place a piece of wax paper around the knife before cutting. Small pieces of wax paper should be placed between each slice of cheese. Cover all parts of the sandwich bread with the cheese. Serve with or without crisp, clean lettuce leaves or other green.

54   American Cheese and Broiled Ham Sandwich

Toast 2 slices of bread and cover with thin, sliced American cheese; place under broiler until cheese begins to melt—about 1½ minutes. Place a slice of broiled ham on top of one-half sandwich before folding. Garnish with a piece of dill.

55   American Cheese Dream Sandwich

Cut bread very thin; spread with butter. Between the slices place thin slices of Swiss cheese, spread with mustard, then minced onion. Garnish with a slice of tomato topped with a slice of dill.

56   American Cheese, Dried Beef and Tomatoes
(Serves 6-8)

Chop fine half a pound of dried beef and mix with a quarter pound grated American cheese. Add a pint of canned tomato soup and cook until thick. When cold use as a filling. Garnish with olive and a slice of green pepper. Keeps well in icebox.

57   American Cheese and Fried Bacon Sandwich

Cover all parts of the sandwich bread with sliced cheese, and cover with thin, crisp fried or broiled bacon.

Top bacon with crisp lettuce leaves. Garnish with a piece of dill pickle, cut fan-like.

58   American Cheese and Green Pepper Sandwich

Combine equal parts of grated American cheese, minced green pepper and chopped stuffed olives. Blend with mayonnaise. Cover sandwich bread with crisp lettuce leaves; over the lettuce, spread the mixture; cover again with crisp lettuce leaves, and top with sandwich bread. Garnish with radish, cut rose-like and a slice of dill pickle.

59   American Cheese and Peanut Butter Sandwich

Spread peanut butter (or apple butter) thinly on a slice of sandwich bread; cover all parts of the sandwich bread with American cheese. Top with another slice of sandwich bread. Cut the sandwich from corner to corner, making 4 triangular small sandwiches. Garnish center with a small bunch of crisp, green watercress, closing the four parts so as to hold the watercress straight, tuff-like. Garnish with a slice of tomato, topped with an olive.

60   American Cheese and Spinach Sandwich

Moisten equal parts of ground American cheese and chopped or ground uncooked spinach with lemon juice and mayonnaise. Spread on any kind of bread. Garnish with a slice of green pepper, crossed with a slice or pimiento.

61   American Cheese and Tomato Sandwich

Cover a piece of sandwich bread (any kind) with thinly sliced American cheese, and place thin slices of tomato on top of the cheese. Cover with crisp lettuce leaves. Top with a slice of the same bread. Cut from corner to corner, making two triangular sandwiches. Serve garnished with celery curls, a sprig of watercress or other green.

62   Camembert Sandwich

Almost any kind of cheese used in sandwich-making, may be changed and camembert used. Always scrape clean camembert cheese before using.

63   Canadian Cheese and Apple Sandwich

Prepare buttered slices from roll loaf. Pare large apples and slice through that each slice may fit on bread; remove the core, and after placing on lower slice of buttered bread, sprinkle blended grated or ground American cheese with mayonnaise. Top with crisp, clean lettuce leaves, then with buttered bread. Garnish with a sweet-sour pickle, a radish and a green olive.

64   Cottage Cheese and Carrot Sandwich

To 1 part of cottage cheese, add 1/3 part of grated raw carrot and 1 scant teaspoon sweet pickles, chopped finely. Season to taste with salt and pepper and spread over sandwich bread, covered with crisp lettuce leaves. Top the cheese with lettuce leaves, and adjust bread sandwich slice. Cut from corner to corner on both way, so as to make four triangular small sandwiches. Garnish with sprig of watercress, and 1 olive.

Chopped nuts may be substituted for sweet pickles, if desired.

65   Cottage Cheese and Cherry Preserves Sandwich

Combine and blend thoroughly equal parts of cottage cheese and well-drained, chopped cherry preserves. Season to taste with a few drops of Worcestershire sauce, salt and pepper. Spread between 2 slices of unbuttered bread (any kind). Cut in two from corner to corner; and garnish with a little shredded red cabbage salad.

66   Cottage Cheese and Cinnamon Sandwich

Put cottage cheese through a sieve; season highly with cinnamon, salt and pepper and a little sugar to taste. Spread between two slices of any kind of bread, preferably rye bread. Garnish with a piece of dill, placed on a small piece of lettuce leaf.

67 Cottage Cheese, Honey and Nuts Sandwich

Butter toasted slices of white or wholewheat bread; lay on each a large lettuce leaf. Spread over the lettuce a spread made of equal parts of cottage cheese, honey and chopped nut meats which should be thoroughly blended. Top with another crisp large lettuce leaf. Top with a toasted slice of bread, and cut diagonally. Garnish with a slice of tomato, placed on a small piece of lettuce.

68 Cottage Cheese and Marmalade Sandwich

Use brown bread. Spread one slice generously with well drained cottage cheese, seasoned to taste with salt, pepper and onion juice. Top with lettuce leaves. Spread another slice of brown bread with any kind of marmalade (orange, pineapple, strawberry, etc.) and adjust over the first slice. Cut from corner to corner, once, then from corner to corner once again. Garnish with a small slice of tomato topped with a slice of hard-cooked egg, again topped with a slice of olive.

69 Cottage Cheese and Olive Sandwiches
(Serves 12 to 15)

To a well drained pound of cottage cheese (2 cups), put through a sieve, add 1 teaspoon Worcestershire sauce, 4 tablespoons chili sauce and 1 cup stoned, chopped ripe olives. Season to taste with salt and white pepper. Spread on buttered Graham bread slices, each slice covered with lettuce leaves. Press gently; cut diagonally; and garnish with 1 radish and a stick of dill pickle.

70 Cottage Cheese and Raisins Sandwich
(Very Popular at Lunch Counters)

To each scant ¼ cup of well-drained, then sieved cottage, add 2 rolled saltines or Graham crackers, 1 scant tablespoon mayonnaise and 1 scant ¼ cup of seedless raisins, chopped very fine or ground. Blend thoroughly and spread between two slices of bread (any kind). Or, split long roll; cover with crisp lettuce and garnish or rather spread mixture between the two slices of roll. Garnish with a little jelly (any kind) placed upon a crisp lettuce leaf.

71   Creamed Cheese

To cream cheese, add drop by drop either a little milk, evaporated milk, or thin cream, blending thoroughly until smooth and free from lumps.

72   Cream Cheese and Almond Sandwiches

This spread keeps well in icebox and may be made in advance. Keep covered with a buttered paper.

1 lb. cream cheese   ½ cup ground blanched almonds
¼ cup pickle relish   ¼ cup celery leaves, ground
        Salt, pepper and paprika to taste
        A dash of Worcestershire sauce

Blend all the above ingredients, and to ensure smoothness, put through food chopper. Serve between slices of whole wheat, raisin, nut or any kind of fruit bread, sliced thin and cut diagonally.

73   Cream Cheese and Apple Sandwich

In this sandwich, large slices of apples, not bread is used.

Rub lemon juice over each side of sliced apples to prevent rusting or browning. Spread with a mixture of creamed cheese and ground nut meats (any kind) or cream cheese and olives, or cream cheese and cress or green pepper, or onion tops. Adjust two apple slices thus spread and dress upon crisp lettuce leaves. Garnish with 1 olive and 1 scant teaspoon of sweet chopped relish.

74   Cream Cheese and Apricot Sandwich

Mix together equal parts of cream cheese and apricot pulp made by pressing through a sieve stewed or canned apricots which have been thoroughly drained. Add mayonnaise to taste, and spread between thin buttered slices of bread covered with crisp lettuce leaves. Nuts may be added if desired. Cut diagonally, and top each part with a slice of hard cooked egg, topped with a caper. Garnish with a scant tablespoon of dressed cole slaw.

75   Cream Cheese and Asparagus Tips Sandwich

Spread creamed cream cheese over plain slices of bread, cover the cheese with a row of asparagus tips, thoroughly drained, and top with a slice of bread. Cut diagonally. Garnish with a cup of lettuce leaves filled with cole slaw sprinkled with minced beets.

76   Cream Cheese and Beet Sandwich

Combine equal parts of creamed cream cheese and cooked beets and blend thoroughly. Spread on slices of bread, covered with lettuce leaves, and top with another slice of bread. Cut diagonally or in small quarters. Garnish with a ripe olive and a small slice of dill pickle.

77   Cream Cheese and Caraway Seeds Sandwiches

Blend to a paste, ¼ lb. cream cheese, ¼ lb. butter and add ½ generous teaspoon of caraway seeds, ½ teaspoon of grated onion and 1½ tablespoons heavy cream. Mix until smooth after seasoning with salt and pepper to taste. Spread between 2 slices of any kind of bread, covered with lettuce leaves. Cut diagonally. Garnish with a stick of dill pickle, placed upon a small piece of lettuce leaf.

Choose different breads when you make sandwiches. Your patrons will have a keener appetite and a greater interest in the whole meal. Corn bread is unusual and delicious for sandwiches, Rye, Whole Wheat, Apricot Bread, Banana Bread, Fig and Nut Bread, Gingerbread, Irish Soda Bread, Sour Milk Spoon Bread, Nut Date Bread, Spiced Corn Bread, Apple Corn Bread, Raisin Bread, Pineapple Honey Bread, Spider Corn Bread, etc., afford varieties, stimulate appetites, thence more sale and more profit.

78   Cream Cheese and Celery Sandwiches

To a pound of cream cheese blend in 1 cup finely chopped celery, using leaves and stalks. Or, the celery may be sprinkled over the cheese when making the sandwich. Cut diagonally; then cut each piece, so as to make 4 small triangular sandwiches. Garnish with 1 olive and 1 piece of dill pickle or sweet-sour gherkin.

79   Cream Cheese, Celery and Cherry Sandwiches

To a pound of cream cheese blend in 2/3 cup chopped celery, using green and stalks and 2/3 cup chopped canned cherries, which have been well-drained. Spread between two slices of bread, covered with shredded lettuce. Cut diagonally. Garnish with a section of orange, placed upon a piece of lettuce leaf.

80   Cream Cheese, Celery and Dates Sandwich

Proceed as indicated for recipe No. 79, substituting dates for cherries.

81 Cream Cheese, Cottage Cheese and Nuts Sandwich

Combine equal parts of cream and cottage cheese, the latter well drained and sieved with equal part of chopped nut meats, adding enough undiluted evaporated milk to make mixture of spreading consistency, and seasoning with salt, pepper and a few drops of Worcestershire sauce to taste. Spread between two slices of corn bread, covered with lettuce leaves. Cut into small squares, and place upon a bed of shredded, dressed lettuce. Garnish with a teaspoon of minced relish, placed upon a small piece of lettuce leaf.

82   Cream Cheese and Cucumber Sandwiches
(Serves 4)

To a package of cream cheese, add enough mayonnaise to make mixture of a spreading consistency, season with salt, coarsely-ground black pepper, a few drops of Tabasco to taste. Spread between two slices of white bread with or without lettuce leaves. Cut diagonally, and top each part with 2 or 3 thin slices of pared cucumber. Garnish with a small stick of dill pickle, placed upon a leaf of lettuce.

83   Cream Cheese and Fig Sandwich

Proceed as indicated for recipe No. 79, substituting figs for cherries.

84   Cream Cheese and Grape Nuts Sandwich

To ¾ parts of cream cheese, add ¼ part of grape nuts (dry breakfast cereal) and 1 teaspoon ground blanched almonds. Salt and pepper to taste, and blend thoroughly. Spread between two slices of any kind of bread, cover with minced red pimiento. Cut diagonally. Garnish with a small stick of canned pineapple, placed upon a piece of lettuce.

85   Cream Cheese and Honey Sandwich

Add enough strained honey to cream cheese, so as to make a mixture of spreading consistency; sprinkle with chopped nut meats. Dress open-faced upon a cold platter. Garnish the other slice of bread with two thin slices of tomatoes. Garnish the plate with 1 black and 1 ripe olive placed upon lettuce leaves.

86   Cream Cheese and Horseradish Sandwich

Combine and blend well equal parts of cream cheese and horseradish; season with salt and pepper to taste; spread between two slices of any kind of bread, covered with crisp lettuce leaves. Cut from corner to corner twice so as to make 4 small triangular sandwiches. Garnish with a slice of apple, dipped in French dressing, dressed upon a lettuce leaf, sprinkled with minced hard-cooked egg, mixed with minced parsley.

87   Cream Cheese and Jelly Sandwich

Spread well creamed cream cheese on 1 slice of

any kind of sandwich bread and any kind of desired jelly on the other slice. Fold together and cut from corner to corner twice, so as to make 4 small triangular sandwiches. Garnish with shredded pineapple, placed upon a crisp lettuce leaf.

88 Cream Cheese and Marmalade Sandwich

Proceed as indicated for recipe No. 87, substituting marmalade (any kind desired) for jelly. Two kinds of bread may be used.

89 Cream Cheese, Horseradish and Nuts Sandwich

Combine and blend thoroughly equal parts each of cream cheese, horseradish and chopped nut meats (any kind). Spread between two slices of any kind of bread. Cut diagonally. Garnish with a plumped prune, the stone of which has been removed, and substituted with a kernel of nut (any kind) then rolled in mixed sugar and cinnamon to taste, placed upon a crisp lettuce leaf.

90 Cream Cheese and Olive Sandwich

After spreading well creamed cream cheese over a slice of sandwich bread, sprinkle with finely chopped olive (any kind). Cover with crisp lettuce leaves. Garnish with a stick of dill pickle.

91 Cream Cheese and Pineapple Sandwich

Combine and blend thoroughly equal parts of creamed cream cheese and well-drained, canned shredded pineapple. Spread between two slices of any kind of bread Cut from corner to corner twice, so as to make 4 small triangular sandwiches. Garnish each small sandwich top with a thin slice of stuffed olive.

92 Cream Cheese, Pimiento and Walnuts Sandwich

Combine and blend well equal parts of creamed cream cheese, minced pimiento and chopped walnuts. Place between two slices of any kind of bread, covered with crisp lettuce leaves. Cut diagonally. Garnish with a stick of canned pineapple placed upon a crisp piece of lettuce leaf.

93 Cream Cheese, Raisin and Green Pepper Sandwiches—(Serves 6)—A Lenten Favorite

Combine and blend thoroughly 2 hard-cooked eggs, riced or sieved, 1 cream cheese, 1 tablespoon minced pimiento and 2 tablespoons of minced green pepper. Season to taste with salt and pepper; spread between two slices of any kind of bread covered with lettuce. Cut from corner to corner so as to form 4 small triangular sandwiches. Garnish with a section of orange, dipped in French dressing, placed upon a piece of crisp lettuce leaf, and a stick of dill pickle.

94 Cream Cheese and Sardine Sandwich
A Lenten Favorite

Combine and blend well equal parts of creamed cream cheese and carefully boned and skinned, well-drained sardines with equal parts of minced olives, salt and pepper to taste and enough French dressing to make mixture of a spreading consistency. Spread between two slices of any kind of bread, thinly spread with anchovy paste. Cut diagonally and garnish with 1 stick of dill placed upon a crisp lettuce leaf.

95 Cream Cheese and Watercress Sandwich

Combine equal parts of creamed cream cheese and finely minced green watercress; season to taste with salt and pepper and a few dashes of Worcestershire sauce. Spread between two slices of bread, with or without lettuce leaves. Cut diagonally. Garnish with a red canned cherry and 1 black olive, placed upon a crisp lettuce leaf. Or, combine equal parts of cream cheese and butter or peanut, or apple butter, and equal parts of finely minced crisp, green watercress. Season to taste with salt and pepper. Cut from corner to corner twice so as to make 4 small triangular sandwiches. Garnish with a stick of dill or a slice of tomato, placed upon crisp lettuce leaf.

96   Deviled Cheese Sandwiches
Cold—(Serves 6)

Use any kind of hard, grating cheese. This mixture keeps well in a jar, when placed in icebox. Whole Wheat, Graham and Brown Bread are the favorites for this mixture.

1 cup grated cheese	½ teaspoon vinegar
¼ teaspoon salt	1 teaspoon peanut butter
1 teaspoon paprika	½ (or more) teaspoon prepared mustard
½ teaspoon Worcestershire sauce	A few grains of cayenne

Combine and blend thoroughly. Spread between two slices of any kind of the indicated bread covered with shredded lettuce. Garnish with sweet-sour gherkin, fan-like, placed upon a crisp lettuce leaf.

97   Edam Cheese Sandwich

May be used instead of American cheese, as indicated for recipe No. 52 up to No. 61 included.

98   French Cream Cheese Sandwich
(Hot)

Make a sandwich in the usual way with well-drained cottage cheese, creamed with enough heavy cream or evaporated milk (undiluted) to a spreading, rather thick consistency, using trimmed French loaf bread. Dip entirely in slightly beaten egg diluted with a little milk and seasoned to taste with salt and pepper and a few grains of nutmeg, and fry in butter until golden browned in butter. Cut crosswise and serve with a spoonful of grape jelly or any other kind of jelly in the center. A good seller.

99   Liederkranz and Catsup Sandwich

Spread slices of rye or pumpernickel bread with butter and then with liederkranz. Cover cheese with thin layer of catsup; cover with another slice of buttered bread. Garnish with stuffed olives.

100 Liederkranz and Onion Sandwich

Spread and mash with a fork a package of liederkranz until it is smooth and soft. Add 2 tablespoons of beer and blend to a smooth paste. Fold in 2 tablespoons of grated or finely minced onion tops or chives or ordinary onion. Spread on buttered rye bread, which may be toasted if desired. Garnish with a stick of dill pickle.

101 Liederkranz and Tomato Sandwich

Spread slices of rye or pumpernickel with Anchovy butter, No. 454, or with Garlic butter, No. 465, or with Mustard butter, No. 475, and then with Liederkranz. Cover the cheese with thin layer of catsup, mixed with a little prepared horseradish. Cover with slices of fresh tomato, and cover with a slice of buttered butter or any of the suggested creamed butters. Cut from corner to corner, so as to make 4 small triangular sandwiches, and place in center a large bunch of crisp, green watercress. Garnish with black olives.

102 Parmesan Cheese and Anchovy Sandwich

To about 3 tablespoons of freshly grated Parmesan cheese, add the size of a peanut or more of anchovy paste, and enough thin cream or evaporated milk to make a spreading paste. Beat well; spread on any kind of bread or toast. Cut diagonally or from corner to corner and garnish with a slice of hard-cooked egg, topped with mayonnaise.

103 Parmesan Cheese and Shrimp Sandwich

To about 3 tablespoons or more of grated Parmesan cheese, add 1 tablespoon of canned, ground or finely chopped shrimps and enough mayonnaise to make a paste of spreading consistency. Spread between two slices of any kind of bread, covered with lettuce leaves. Cut diagonally. Garnish with 1 olive, pitted, stuffed with 1 whole shrimp rolled in mayonnaise.

104 Parmesan Cheese and Tomato Paste Sandwich

To about 3 tablespoons of grated Parmesan cheese, add and blend well 1 tablespoon of tomato catsup and 1 tablespoon of tomato paste. Spread on a slice of bread or toast; sprinkle with minced peanuts; cover with lettuce leaves; then adjust another slice of bread or toast. Cut from corner to corner so as to make 4 small triangular sandwiches, each topped with a slice of broiled tomato. Garnish with celery curls, or a strip of red pimiento.

105 Pimiento Cheese and Deviled Ham Sandwiches
(Serves 8-10)

Combine 1 can deviled ham with 1 cup pimiento cheese, 1 tablespoon prepared mustard, and ½ cup of peanut butter. Blend well; spread between slices of any kind of bread, covered with minced or shredded lettuce. Cut diagonally, and top each part with a slice of cucumber, topped itself with a slice of beet.

106   Pimiento Cheese and Watercress Sandwich

Combine equal parts of pimiento cheese, mustard butter and minced watercress, and spread between two slices of any kind of bread. Garnish with a tablespoon of dressed cole slaw.

107   Roquefort Cheese and Chicken Sandwich

Butter or rather spread mustard butter over two slices of untoasted bread; cover the cheese with thin slices of cooked chicken and adjust another piece of bread over, also spread with mustard butter. Cut diagonally, and top each part with a slice of tomato.

108   Roquefort Cheese, Caviar, Egg and Tomato Sandwich

Arrange on 1 slice of rye bread, creamed Roquefort cheese on half of the slice and sliced tomato on the other half part. On another slice of rye bread or pumpernickel bread, arrange caviar on a tiny lettuce cup, and chopped, hard-cooked eggs on the other half part. Dress upon a chilled platter, open, and garnished with a small lettuce cup filled with minced, finely chopped onion, sprinkled with a little paprika.

109 Roquefort Cheese and Worcestershire Sauce Sandwich

Cream about 2 tablespoons of Roquefort cheese with a generous dash of Worcestershire sauce; spread over freshly made toast; cover with a piece of toast, and cut from corner to corner so as to make 4 triangular sandwiches (small). Serve garnished with a small lettuce cup filled with drained, shredded pineapple (canned).

110 Schnitzelbank Cheese Pot Sandwiches
(Serves 30)

This great favorite among German folks who eat while singing "Ei du schöne, ei du schöne, ei du schöne Schnitzelbank" and drink many steins of beer, has the great advantage that the longer it is kept in a crock jar, the better it will be. Of course rye or pumpernickel bread, cut into thin slices is here indicated.

Scrape clean and free from outer skin two camemberts and one Liederkranz cheeses and put in a copper or enamel pot with 1 quarter pound of Roquefort cheese, ½ lb. butter, 2 tablespoons flour and 1 pint of cream. Boil this till melted into a smooth mass. Strain through a cheese cloth or sieve and then into this mix 1 cup of finely chopped olive meat and ½ cup pimiento. Season highly with salt, pepper and cayenne. Pack into a crock jar and let cool. Spread between two thin slices of either pumpernickel (rye, well-seeded, may be used) and cut from corner to corner so as to make 4 small triangular sandwiches. Garnish with generous sticks of dill pickles and a little cole slaw placed upon crisp lettuce leaf.

111 Swiss Cheese and Asparagus Sandwich

Drain canned asparagus tips well before using on sandwich bread; cover with green lettuce leaves; top with sliced thin Swiss cheese. Cut diagonally. Garnish with sweet-sour or dill pickle placed upon crisp lettuce leaf.

112   Swiss Cheese and Bacon Sandwich

Arrange asparagus tips upon slice of bread, covered with crisp lettuce leaves. Top asparagus with broiled bacon strips. On the other slice of bread (any kind) arrange thin slices of Swiss cheese. Serve open-faced, garnished with a thin slice of tomato, topped with a stick of dill pickle. You may spread the bread with prepared mustard, if desired.

113   Swiss Cheese and Cole Slaw Sandwich

Spread evenly cole slaw between two slices of any kind of bread and top with thin slices of Swiss cheese. Cut diagonally. Garnish with 1 olive and 1 radish.

114   Swiss Cheese, Corned Beef and Bologna Sandwich

A real he-man sandwich which should bring a good price.

Arrange alternate layers of Swiss cheese, shredded lettuce, then thinly sliced corned beef and shredded lettuce. Top with thinly sliced Bologna sausage; then with shredded lettuce. Cut sandwich diagonally. Top each part with a stick of dill pickle, and garnish with a slice of tomato placed upon a crisp lettuce leaf.

115   Swiss Cheese and Crabmeat Sandwich

Spread well-seasoned crab flake salad (French dressing or mayonnaise may be used) between two slices of freshly made toast. Top the crabmeat with thin slices of Swiss cheese. Cut from corner to corner, so as to make 4 small triangular sandwiches. Garnish with olive and a thin slice of lemon, placed upon crisp lettuce leaf.

116   Swiss Cheese and Egg Sandwich

May be served open-faced or closed and cut triangularly or into 4 small triangular pieces. Place thin slices of Swiss cheese between two slices of any kind of bread which may be spread with prepared mustard, mustard butter (No. 475) or horseradish butter (No. 468). Top Swiss cheese with sliced hard-cooked eggs; cover the egg slices with crisp green lettuce leaves. Cut diagonally. Garnish with a dill pickle stick and 1 olive.

117   Swiss Cheese and Ham Sandwich

Arrange upon 1 slice of bread spread with mustard or mustard butter (No. 475) thin slices of Swiss cheese. Cover with crisp lettuce leaves, then with thin slice of cold cooked ham. Top with a slice of sandwich bread, also spread with mustard or mustard butter. Cut from corner to corner so as to make 4 small triangular sandwiches or diagonally. Garnish with a little horseradish placed upon a small piece of lettuce leaf.

118   Swiss Cheese and Liverwurst Sandwich

Proceed as indicated for recipe No. 117, Swiss Cheese and Ham, substituting liverwurst for ham.

119   Swiss Cheese and Potato Salad Sandwich

Proceed as indicated for recipe No. 117, Swiss Cheese and Ham, substituting Potato salad for Ham.

120   Swiss Cheese and Pork Sandwich

Proceed as indicated for recipe No. 117, Swiss Cheese and Ham, substituting cold cooked pork for ham.

121   Swiss Cheese and Roastbeef Sandwich

Proceed as indicated for recipe No. 117, Swiss Cheese and Ham, substituting cold cooked roastbeef for ham.

122   Swiss Cheese and Salami Sandwich

Proceed as indicated for recipe No. 117, Swiss Cheese and Ham, substituting Salami for Ham. Salami may be mashed or left whole.

123   Swiss Cheese and Tongue Sandwich

Proceed as indicated for recipe No. 117, Swiss Cheese and Ham, substituting tongue for ham.

124   Swiss Cheese and Tomato Sandwich

Proceed as indicated for recipe No. 117, Swiss Cheese and Ham, substituting thinly sliced tomato for ham.

125   Swiss Cheese and Turkey Sandwich

Proceed as indicated for recipe No. 117, Swiss Cheese and Ham, substituting cold cooked, thinly sliced turkey (or chicken) for ham. Garnish with a teaspoon of cranberry sauce placed upon a small piece of lettuce leaf.

CLUB OR THREE-DECKER COMBINATION SANDWICHES

126   Club or Three-Decker Sandwiches

Club or Three-Decker Sandwiches are made of three slices of bread which may be plain, toasted, buttered, or spread with a creamed (compounded) butter; served cold or hot. They may be cut in halves, from corner to corner, that is, diagonally, in thirds, or quarters.

First the lower layer is filled with a spread or a filling, topped with another slice of bread or toast, also filled with a spread or a filling, and finally topped with a plain or toasted slice of bread; gently pressed together with the tips of the fingers and the sandwich knife, then cut according to order or fancy as indicated above. When cut in thirds or quarters, they may be held together with toothpicks. At any rate, hot club or three-decker sandwiches should be served upon hot plate or kept for a short while on the hot steam table. Both hot or cold club or three-decker sandwiches, and in fact any kind of sandwich, should be daintily, soberly garnished before being presented to patrons.

The following recipes, ideas and suggestions for Club or Three-Decker Sandwiches are sufficiently clear so as to eliminate further details and explanations; furthermore, they are not rigid prescriptions, and are sufficiently elastic so as to allow all the changes which may be required by circumstances and size of the business. Above all, these recipes, ideas and formulas are concise, practical and economical, and to facilitate research and eliminate loss of time, they are all numbered and classified alphabetically, the main ingredient for each layer, being printed in capital letters, so that at a glance the chef will find immediately what he is looking for and be able to solve the important problem of "Speed Element" so prominently necessary and identified with the present day Menu Problem.

Perhaps you may notice that no mention is made of removing the crusts from the bread. This may be done if the sandwiches are to be served for tea, but these club and three-decker sandwiches being almost a meal, many patrons require the crust on, as it provides a delicate flavor which is worth preserving when these sandwiches are used for lunch or supper. Mayonnaise may be used instead of butter as a spread for the bread.

127   Apricot-Ham on Toast

Lower Layer—Cooked, sieved APRICOTS, covered with lettuce.

Second Layer—Cold cooked HAM, covered with lettuce and mayonnaise.

128   Almond-Peanut Butter on Toast

LL—SHREDDED ALMOND, mixed with COTTAGE CHEESE and JELLY.

SL—PEANUT BUTTER and lettuce.

129   Almond-Pineapple on Bread

LL—ALMOND BUTTER, lettuce.

SL—PINEAPPLE slice, lettuce spread with mayonnaise.

130   Almond-Marmalade on Toast
LL—ALMOND BUTTER and MARMALADE, lettuce.
SL—SLICED ORANGES and lettuce.

**131   Almond-Marshmallow-Fig Date Filling
on Toast or Bread**
LL—ALMOND BUTTER—chopped and melted MARSHMALLOW and lettuce.
SL—FIG DATE FILLING and shredded lettuce.

132   American Cheese-Ham and Tomato on Toast
LL—AMERICAN CHEESE and lettuce with mayonnaise.
SL—GRILLED HAM, topped with TOMATO SLICES and lettuce.

**133   American Cheese-Peanut Butter and Jelly
on Bread**
LL—AMERICAN CHEESE, lettuce and mustard mayonnaise.
SL—Bread spread with PEANUT BUTTER, then with JELLY, then with lettuce.

**134   Apple-Peanut Butter Filling and Pineapple
Slice on Toast**
LL—SLICED APPLE-PEANUT BUTTER FILLING and shredded lettuce.
SL—PINEAPPLE SLICE and shredded lettuce.

135 Apple-Nut-Fig and Shredded Pineapple on Rye
LL—SLICED APPLE-NUT and FIG, chopped and shredded lettuce with mayonnaise.
SL—SHREDDED PINEAPPLE and shredded lettuce with mayonnaise.

**136   Asparagus Tips-Tomato and Cole Slaw
on Whole Wheat**
LL—ASPARAGUS TIPS covered with SLICED TOMATOES.
SL—COLE SLAW dressed with mayonnaise.

137   Bacon and Banana on Toast
LL—BROILED BACON (2 slices) on toast covered with horseradish, butter, lettuce.
SL—SLICED BANANA on toast buttered with peanut butter, dressed lettuce with mayonnaise.

138 Bacon-Orange Marmalade and Banana on Rye
LL—BROILED BACON covered with lettuce.
SL—Rye bread spread with ORANGE MARMALADE, then with SLICED BANANA, covered with lettuce.

139   Bacon-Bean Salad and Tomato on White
LL—BROILED BACON over lettuce, covered with BEAN SALAD.
SL—SLICED TOMATOES covered with lettuce.

140   Bacon-Chicken and Anchovies on Toast
LL—BROILED BACON, covered with lettuce.
SL—SLICED CHICKEN, covered with ANCHOVY filets, then with SLICED TOMATOES and lettuce.

141   Bacon-Chicken-Green Pepper and Tomato on Toast
LL—BROILED BACON, covered with SLICED CHICKEN, then with lettuce.
SL—GREEN PEPPER SLICES and SLICED TOMATOES.

142   Bacon-Green Pepper and Tomato on Toast
LL—BROILED BACON, covered with GREEN PEPPER Slices.
SL—Cole slaw and SLICED TOMATO.

143   Bacon-Chicken Livers and Tomato on Toast
LL—BROILED BACON covered with BROILED CHICKEN LIVERS.
SL—SLICED TOMATOES covered with watercress.

144   Bacon-Onion and Tomato on Rye
LL—BROILED BACON covered with thinly sliced raw ONION covered with lettuce.
SL—SLICED TOMATOES covered with watercress.

145 Bacon-Potato Salad and Tomato on Rye

LL—BROILED BACON covered with hot POTATO SALAD.
SL—SLICED TOMATOES covered with cole slaw.

146 Bacon-Potato Salad and Egg Salad on White

LL—BROILED BACON covered with hot POTATO SALAD.
SL—EGG SALAD covered with lettuce.

147 Bacon-Potato Salad and Ham on Toast

LL—BROILED BACON covered with cold POTATO SALAD, then with lettuce.
SL—Thinly SLICED HAM covered with lettuce and mayonnaise.

148 Bacon-Swiss Cheese and Egg-Anchovy on Toast

LL—BROILED BACON covered with thin slice of SWISS CHEESE then with lettuce or watercress.
SL—SLICED HARD-COOKED EGGS and ANCHOVY FILETS, covered with shredded lettuce.

149 Bacon-Tomato and Onion-Caviar on Toast

LL—BROILED BACON covered with SLICED TOMATOES.
SL—Thinly SLICED ONION (raw) covered with CAVIAR, then with lettuce.

150 Bacon-Swiss Cheese and Turkey on Toasted Rye

LL—BROILED BACON, covered with thin slices of SWISS CHEESE, spread with prepared mustard.
SL—SLICED TURKEY covered with watercress and mayonnaise.

151 Bacon-Swiss Cheese and Tongue-Tomato on White

LL—BROILED BACON, covered with thinly SLICED SWISS CHEESE.

SL—SLICED TONGUE covered with TOMATO, then with lettuce.

152 Bacon-Tomato and Sardine on Rye

LL—BROILED BACON covered with SLICED TOMATOES.
SL—Spread with anchovy paste, covered with whole SARDINES then with lettuce.

153 Bacon-Tomato and Liverwurst on White

LL—BROILED BACON covered with SLICED TOMATOES and cress.
SL—Thinly sliced LIVERWURST, covered with cole slaw.

154 Bacon-Cress and Salami on White

LL—BROILED BACON covered with watercress.
SL—Sliced SALAMI covered with vegetable salad and lettuce.

155 Bacon-Cucumber and Asparagus Tips on Rye

LL—BROILED BACON covered with CUCUMBER slices and lettuce.
SL—Spread with dressed shredded lettuce; covered with ASPARAGUS TIPS dipped in French dressing.

156 Bacon-Tomato-Cole Slaw and Swiss Cheese on Toast

LL—BROILED BACON covered with TOMATO slices, then with COLE SLAW.
SL—Thinly sliced SWISS CHEESE covered with mustard, then with lettuce.

157 Bacon-Tomato and Vegetable Salad on Whole Wheat

LL—BROILED BACON covered with TOMATO SLICES.
SL—Covered with lettuce leaves, then with VEGETABLE SALAD.

158   Bacon-Watercress and Beef Salad on Rye

LL—BROILED BACON covered with watercress.
SL—Covered with lettuce, then with BEEF SALAD.

**159   Beef Salad-Cole Slaw and Tomato
on White**

LL—Covered with lettuce leaves, then with BEEF SALAD and covered with COLE SLAW.
SL—TOMATO Slices covered with lettuce.

**160 Beef Salad-Pickle Relish and American Cheese
on White**

LL—Covered with lettuce, then with BEEF SALAD and PICKLE.
SL—Covered with watercress, then with sliced AMERICAN CHEESE.

161   Caviar-Onion and Tomato on Toast

LL—Covered with a layer of CAVIAR then topped with SLICED ONIONS.
SL—TOMATO SLICES covered with watercress.

**162   Chicken-Bacon and Tomato-Olives
on White**

LL—SLICED CHICKEN covered with BROILED BACON.
SL—SLICED TOMATOES covered with chopped OLIVES and lettuce.

**163   Chicken-Celery-Lettuce and Bacon-Tomato
on Rye**

LL—SLICED CHICKEN covered with small CELERY stalks, then with lettuce.
SL—BROILED BACON and TOMATO SLICES.

**164   Chicken-Bacon and Green Pepper-Tomato
on Toast**

LL—SLICED CHICKEN covered with BROILED BACON and lettuce.
SL—GREEN PEPPER SLICES covered with TOMATO SLICES.

**165   Chicken-Lettuce and Jelly-Cress
on Raisin Bread**

LL—SLICED CHICKEN covered with lettuce leaves.
SL—Spread with JELLY (any kind) and covered with chopped watercress.

**166   Chicken-Nut Meats and Jelly-Lettuce
on Pumpernickel**

LL—Spread with SLICED CHICKEN, then covered with NUT MEATS mixed with a little mayonnaise.
SL—Spread with JELLY (any kind) mixed with chopped lettuce.

**167   Chicken-Asparagus Tips and Bacon-Tomato
on Toast**

LL—Spread with SLICED CHICKEN, then covered with canned ASPARAGUS TIPS.
SL—Covered with BROILED BACON, SLICED TOMATOES and lettuce.

**168   Chicken-Bacon and Tomato-Nut Meats
on Rye**

LL—Covered with SLICED CHICKEN, then topped with BROILED BACON.
SL—Covered with TOMATO SLICES, then with chopped nut meats and covered with lettuce leaves.

**169   Chicken-Green Pepper and Tomato-Anchovy
on Rye**

LL—Covered with SLICED CHICKEN, then topped with chopped GREEN PEPPER and broiled bacon.
SL—Covered with TOMATO SLICES, topped with 2 ANCHOVY FILETS, covered with lettuce leaves.

**170   Chicken-Bacon and Tongue-Tomato
on Whole Wheat**

LL—Covered with SLICED CHICKEN, then with BROILED BACON.
SL—Covered with cold, SLICED TONGUE, TOMATO SLICES and lettuce leaves.

**171 Chicken Salad and Tomato-Tongue
on Boston Brown Bread**

LL—Covered with CHICKEN SALAD, then with shredded lettuce.

SL—Covered with cold cooked, SLICED TONGUE, TOMATO SLICES and lettuce leaves.

**172 Chicken Salad and Ham-Swiss Cheese
on Pumpernickel**

LL—Covered with CHICKEN SALAD, then with lettuce leaves.

SL—Covered with thin slice of HAM, topped with thin slices of cold cooked TONGUE.

**173 Chicken Salad-Tomato and Anchovy-Lettuce
on Rye**

LL—Covered with CHICKEN SALAD, then topped with TOMATO SLICES.

SL—Covered with FILET of ANCHOVIES, then with shredded lettuce.

**174 Chicken Salad-Bacon and Tomato-Relish
on Nut Bread**

LL—Covered with CHICKEN SALAD, then with 2 slices of BACON.

SL—Covered with TOMATO SLICES, then topped with chopped relish (any kind), lastly covered with lettuce leaves.

**175 Chicken Salad-Tomato and Asparagus Tips
on White**

LL—Covered with CHICKEN SALAD, then with TOMATO SLICES.

SL—Covered with ASPARAGUS TIPS, then with shredded lettuce.

**176 Chicken Salad-Green Pepper and Swiss Cheese-
Tomato on Toasted Rye**

LL—Covered with CHICKEN SALAD, then with chopped GREEN PEPPER.

SL—Covered with thinly SLICED SWISS CHEESE, topped with SLICED TOMATOES, then covered with lettuce leaves.

177   Chicken Salad-Olives and American Cheese-Tomato on Toast

LL—Covered with CHICKEN SALAD, topped with chopped, pitted OLIVES, then with lettuce leaves.

SL—Covered with thin slices of AMERICAN CHEESE, then with TOMATO SLICES, and covered with lettuce leaves.

178   Chicken Salad-Pimientos and Roast Beef-Pickle on Toast

LL—Covered with CHICKEN SALAD, topped with chopped PIMIENTOS, then with chopped watercress.

SL—Covered with cold ROAST BEEF, topped with chopped PICKLES, topped with lettuce leaves.

179   Chicken Salad-Beets and Tongue-Tomato on White

LL—Covered with CHICKEN SALAD, topped with chopped SPICED BEETS, then with lettuce.

SL—Covered with thin slices of TONGUE, topped with thinly SLICED TOMATOES, and topped with lettuce leaves.

180   Chicken Salad-Cole Slaw and Ham-Tomato on Toasted Rye

LL—Covered with CHICKEN SALAD, then with COLE SLAW.

SL—Covered with thinly SLICED BOILED HAM, topped with TOMATO SLICES, then with lettuce leaves.

181   Chicken Salad-Tomato and Vegetable Salad on Toast

LL—Covered with CHICKEN SALAD, then with TOMATO SLICES, topped with shredded lettuce.

SL—Covered with VEGETABLE SALAD, then with lettuce leaves.

182 Chicken Salad-Cucumber and Cream Cheese-Anchovy on Pumpernickel

LL—Covered with CHICKEN SALAD, topped with SLICED CUCUMBER then with lettuce leaves.

SL—Covered with CREAM CHEESE, topped with 3 FILETS of ANCHOVY, topped with lettuce leaves.

183 Chicken-Lettuce and Egg-Lettuce on White

LL—Covered with SLICED CHICKEN, then with shredded lettuce mixed with mayonnaise.

SL—Covered with EGG, then with lettuce leaves.

184 Chicken-Lettuce and Pineapple-Red Cabbage on Toast

LL—Covered with SLICED CHICKEN, then covered with lettuce leaves.

SL—Covered with drained, canned, shredded PINEAPPLE then with shredded RED CABBAGE and covered with lettuce leaves.

185 Chicken Livers-Bacon and Tomato on Nut Bread

LL—Covered with SAUTEED CHICKEN LIVERS, then with BROILED BACON, topped with lettuce leaves.

SL—Covered with lettuce, then with TOMATO SLICES.

186 Chicken Livers-Red Cole Slaw and Tomato on Raisin Bread

LL—Covered with BROILED CHICKEN LIVERS, then topped with RED COLE SLAW.

SL—Covered with TOMATO SLICES, then topped with chopped watercress mixed with mustard mayonnaise.

187 Chicken Livers-Fried Tomato and Bacon-Cucumber on Toast

LL—Covered with broiled, then mashed CHICKEN LIVERS, covered with broiled TOMATO slices, topped with lettuce leaves.

SL—Covered with lettuce leaves, then with broiled BACON, and topped with sliced CUCUMBER, covered with lettuce.

188 Corned Beef-Cole Slaw and Tomato-Lettuce on White

LL—Covered with thinly sliced cold, cooked CORNED BEEF, then topped with seasoned COLE SLAW.

SL—Covered with TOMATO slices, then covered with lettuce leaves.

189 Corned Beef-Horseradish and Tomato Cress on White

LL—Covered with thin slices of cold, cooked CORNED BEEF, then topped with prepared HORSERADISH.

SL—Covered with sliced TOMATOES, covered with mayonnaise, then topped with lettuce leaves.

190 Corned Beef-Dill and Pickled Beets-Lettuce on Rye

LL—Covered with thinly sliced, cold, cooked, lean, CORNED BEEF, covered with thin slices of DILL PICKLES, then topped with lettuce leaves.

SL—Covered with sliced PICKLED BEETS (well-drained) and topped with seasoned, shredded lettuce.

191 Corned Beef-Apple and American Cheese-Lettuce on Toasted Raisin Bread

LL—Covered with thinly sliced, cold, cooked CORNED BEEF, topped with slices of COOKING APPLES, slightly spread with prepared mustard, then topped with lettuce leaves.

SL—Covered with AMERICAN CHEESE, then topped with lettuce.

192 Corned Beef-Onion Slices and Swiss Cheese-Cress on Toasted Rye

LL—Covered with thinly sliced, cold, cooked CORNED BEEF, spread with prepared mustard (slightly), covered with ONION SLICES (very thin), then topped with lettuce.

SL—Covered with thinly sliced SWISS CHEESE, topped with chopped CRESS mixed with mustard mayonnaise.

193   Corned Beef-Cabbage Relish and Pineapple-Lettuce on Toast

LL—Covered with thinly sliced, cold, cooked CORNED BEEF, .covered with CABBAGE RELISH.

SL—Covered with well-drained crushed PINEAPPLE, topped with lettuce leaves.

194   Corned Beef-Chopped Spinach and Cream Cheese on Whole Wheat

LL—Covered with thinly sliced, cold, cooked CORNED BEEF, then topped with raw, CHOPPED SPINACH.

SL—Covered with CREAM CHEESE, mixed with equal parts of shredded lettuce or cabbage.

195   Crab Meat-Olives and Tomato-Lettuce on Nut Bread

LL—Covered with flaked, boned, canned CRAB MEAT, dressed with catsup and pitted, chopped black OLIVES, topped with lettuce leaves.

SL—Covered with TOMATO SLICES spread with a little prepared mustard, then topped with shredded lettuce.

196   Crab Meat Mayonnaise-Tomato and Egg Salad-Cress on Toast

LL—Covered with CRAB MEAT dressed with mayonnaise, then topped with TOMATO SLICES.

SL—Covered with EGG SALAD, topped with WATERCRESS.

197   Crab Meat Mayonnaise-Cucumber and Tomato-Lettuce on Toasted Rye

LL—Covered with CRAB MEAT MAYONNAISE (to which may be added a little catsup or tomato paste), topped with CUCUMBER SLICES, covered with lettuce leaves.

SL—Covered with TOMATO SLICES, topped with lettuce leaves.

198 Crab Meat Mayonnaise-Tomato and Dill-Lettuce on Raisin Bread

LL—Covered with CRAB MEAT MAYONNAISE (to which may be added capers and mustard), topped with TOMATO SLICES then with lettuce leaves.

SL—Covered with sliced DILL PICKLES (lengthwise), topped with shredded, dressed lettuce.

199 Crab Meat-Nut Mayonnaise and Tongue-Lettuce on Toast

LL—Covered with Crab Meat and Nut Meats (chopped coarsely) and mixed with mayonnaise, topped with lettuce leaves.

SL—Covered with thinly sliced, cold, cooked TONGUE, then topped with dressed lettuce leaves.

200 Crab Meat-Raw Spinach and Egg Salad-Lettuce on White

LL—Covered with CRAB MEAT MAYONNAISE, then topped with chopped RAW SPINACH.

SL—Covered with EGG SALAD (mayonnaise), then topped with lettuce leaves.

201 Crab Meat Mayonnaise and String Beans Salad-Lettuce on Toast

LL—Covered with CRAB MEAT MAYONNAISE, topped with sliced onion (very thinly sliced), topped with lettuce leaves.

SL—Covered with STRING BEANS SALAD (French dressing), topped with lettuce leaves.

202 Crab Meat and Shrimp Mayonnaise and Vegetable Salad on Toasted Rye

LL—Covered with CRAB MEAT and SHRIMP MAYONNAISE, topped with shredded red cabbage.

SL—Covered with VEGETABLE SALAD (French dressing), topped with lettuce leaves. (A fine sandwich, when made on Boston Brown bread.)

203 Crab Meat and Apple Mayonnaise and Sliced Pineapple on Toasted Raisin Bread

LL—Covered with CRAB MEAT and APPLE (cubed small) MAYONNAISE, topped with thinly sliced onion.

SL—Covered with PINEAPPLE slice, then topped with lettuce.

204 Crab Meat Mayonnaise and Baked Beans Salad on Whole Wheat

LL—Covered with CRAB MEAT MAYONNAISE, topped with shredded raw white or red cabbage.

SL—Covered with BAKED BEANS (cold) SALAD (French dressing) topped with lettuce leaves.

205 Crab Meat Mayonnaise and Cucumber-Cress on Toast

LL—Covered with CRAB MEAT MAYONNAISE, then with lettuce leaves.

SL—Covered first with peanut butter, then with thin slices of CUCUMBER, and topped with crisp, green WATERCRESS.

206 Crab Meat Mayonnaise and Salmon-Lettuce on White

LL—Covered with CRAB MEAT MAYONNAISE, then covered with olive slices, topped with lettuce leaves.

SL—Covered with flaked, canned SALMON, slightly (gently) mixed with horseradish, then topped with lettuce leaves.

207 Crab Meat Curried Mayonnaise and Sardine-Lettuce on Toasted Rye

LL—Covered with CRAB MEAT mixed with CURRIED MAYONNAISE, then topped with shredded red cabbage.

SL—Covered with skinned, boned SARDINES, then topped with lettuce leaves.

208 Crab Meat-Ham Mayonnaise and Banana-Lettuce on White

LL—Covered with mixed CRAB MEAT and HAM (in

equal parts) dressed with mayonnaise, then topped with shredded lettuce.

SL—Covered with BANANA (sprinkled with lemon juice), then topped with shredded raw spinach, dressed with French dressing.

209   Date and Nut Meats, Mayonnaise and Ham-Lettuce on Toast

LL—Covered with chopped DATES and NUT MEATS (any kind) mixed with mayonnaise, then topped with lettuce leaves.

SL—Covered first with mustard (prepared), then with a thin slice of cold, boiled HAM, and topped with shredded cress.

210   Date, Cherry, Pineapple, Nut Mayonnaise-and Toasted Marshmallow-Shredded Coconut on Toasted Rye

LL—Covered with a salad made of equal parts of pitted, chopped DATES, pitted, canned CHERRIES, shredded, well-drained PINEAPPLE (canned), and chopped NUT MEATS (any kind), mixed with mayonnaise, then topped with lettuce leaves.

SL—Covered with TOASTED MARSHMALLOW, sprinkled with shredded COCONUT, topped with lettuce leaves.

211   Date, Peanut, Apple Mayonnaise and Pineapple-Cress on White

LL—Covered with pitted, chopped DATES, chopped PEANUTS, and cubed, pared, cooking APPLES, mixed with mayonnaise, then topped with lettuce leaves.

SL—Covered with a slice of PINEAPPLE, then topped with (and generously) crisp WATERCRESS sprigs.

212   Deviled Egg-Sardine Salad and Tomato-Lettuce on Boston Brown Bread

LL—Covered with DEVILED EGG, then with SARDINE SALAD.

SL—Covered with TOMATO SLICES, topped with lettuce leaves.

213 Deviled Egg-Sardine Salad and Bacon-Tomato on Pumpernickel

LL—Covered with DEVILED EGG, then with SARDINE SALAD, topped with lettuce leaves.

SL—Covered with broiled BACON, then with TOMATO SLICES; and topped with WATERCRESS.

214 Deviled Egg-Salmon Salad and Green Pepper-Lettuce on Toast

LL—Covered with DEVILED EGG, then with SALMON SALAD, topped with lettuce leaves.

SL—Covered with GREEN PEPPER rings, then with shredded lettuce.

215 Deviled Egg-Crab Meat Salad and Green Onion (sliced thin) or Scallions-Lettuce on Toast

LL—Covered with DEVILED EGG, then with CRAB MEAT SALAD.

SL—Covered with either GREEN ONION (sliced thin) or SCALLIONS, then topped with lettuce leaves.

216 Deviled Egg-Shrimp Salad and Tongue-Cress on Toast

LL—Covered with DEVILED EGG, then with SHRIMP SALAD.

SL—Covered with thinly sliced TONGUE, topped with seasoned WATERCRESS.

217 Deviled Egg-Chicken Salad and Spanish Onion-Cress on Toast

LL—Covered with DEVILED EGG, then with CHICKEN SALAD, topped with lettuce leaves.

SL—Covered with thinly sliced SPANISH ONION, then topped with crisp, green WATERCRESS.

218 Egg Salad-Watercress and Anchovy-Bacon-Lettuce on White

LL—Covered with EGG SALAD, then topped with chopped WATERCRESS.

SL—Covered with filets of ANCHOVY, then with broiled BACON and topped with lettuce leaves.

219 Egg Salad-Green Pepper and Tomato-Anchovy-Lettuce on Whole Wheat

LL—Covered with EGG SALAD, then with GREEN PEPPER rings.

SL—Covered with TOMATO slices, ANCHOVY filets, and topped with lettuce leaves.

220 Egg Salad-Asparagus Tips and Ham-Cheese-Lettuce on Whole Wheat

LL—Covered with EGG SALAD, then topped with ASPARAGUS tips.

SL—Covered with a thin slice of HAM, covered with a thin slice of AMERICAN CHEESE, topped with shredded lettuce.

221 Egg Salad-Chopped Olives and Tomato-Anchovy-Lettuce on Toast

LL—Covered with EGG SALAD, topped with CHOPPED OLIVES.

SL—Covered with TOMATO slices, then with ANCHOVY filets, and topped with lettuce leaves.

222 Egg Salad-Tongue and American Cheese-Lettuce on Rye

LL—Covered with EGG SALAD, topped with thinly sliced, cold, cooked TONGUE.

SL—Covered with AMERICAN CHEESE, spread with prepared mustard, and topped with lettuce leaves.

223 Egg Salad-Ham and Tomato-Lettuce or Cress on Toasted Roll

LL—Covered with EGG SALAD, topped with lettuce leaves.

SL—Covered with TOMATO slices, and topped with either lettuce leaves or watercress.

224 Egg Salad-Roast Beef and Tomato-Anchovy-Lettuce on White

LL—Covered with EGG SALAD, then covered with

cold ROAST BEEF, and topped with lettuce leaves.

SL—Covered with TOMATO slices, then with ANCHOVY filets, and topped with lettuce leaves.

225   Egg Salad-Roast Pork and Tomato-Lettuce on White

LL—Covered with EGG SALAD, then with a thin slice of cold ROAST PORK, and topped with lettuce leaves.

SL—Covered with TOMATO slices, and topped with lettuce leaves.

226   Egg Salad-Sardines-Cress and Tomato-Lettuce on Toast

LL—Covered with EGG SALAD, then covered with mashed SARDINES and topped with crisp WATERCRESS.

SL—Covered with TOMATO slices spread with prepared mustard, and topped with lettuce leaves.

227   Egg Salad-Green Pepper Rings and Sardines-Nut Meats on Whole Wheat

LL—Covered with EGG SALAD, then topped with GREEN PEPPER RINGS.

SL—Covered with whole SARDINES (split in two), then with chopped NUT MEATS (any kind), mixed with mayonnaise, and topped with lettuce leaves.

228   Egg Salad-Tomato and Salmon-Olive Meats-Lettuce on Toasted Rye

LL—Covered with EGG SALAD, then topped with TOMATO slices.

SL—Covered with flaked SALMON mixed with French dressing and chopped OLIVES, then covered with lettuce leaves.

229   Egg Salad-Pimientos and Chicken-Bacon-Lettuce on Toast

LL—Covered with EGG SALAD, then with chopped PIMIENTOS, and lettuce leaves.

SL—Covered with sliced CHICKEN, then with broiled BACON, and topped with lettuce leaves.

230 Egg Salad-Bacon and Tomato-Green Pepper-Lettuce on Toast

LL—Covered with EGG SALAD, then with broiled BACON, and topped with lettuce leaves.

SL—Covered with TOMATO slices, spread with prepared mustard, then covered with GREEN PEPPER RINGS, and topped with lettuce leaves.

231 Egg Salad-Minced Ham and Liverwurst-Tomato-Lettuce on Pumpernickel

LL—Covered with EGG SALAD, then with minced, cold HAM, and topped with shredded lettuce.

SL—Covered with thinly sliced LIVERWURST, then with TOMATO slices, and topped with lettuce leaves.

232 Egg Salad-Bacon and Tomato Anchovy Filets-Lettuce on Boston Brown Bread

LL—Covered with EGG SALAD, then with BACON, and topped with lettuce leaves.

SL—Covered with sliced TOMATOES, then with ANCHOVY filets, and topped with lettuce leaves.

233 Egg Salad-Bacon and Swiss Cheese-Cress on White

LL—Covered with EGG SALAD, then with broiled BACON, and topped with lettuce leaves.

SL—Covered with SWISS CHEESE, spread (slightly) with prepared mustard, then topped with crisp WATERCRESS.

234 Egg Salad-Bologna and Tomato-Lettuce on Rye

LL—Covered with EGG SALAD, then with thin slice of BOLOGNA, and topped with shredded watercress.

SL—Covered with TOMATO slices, spread with prepared mustard (slightly) and topped with lettuce leaves.

**235   Egg Salad-Bacon and Tomato-Anchovy-Lettuce
on Toasted Whole Wheat**

LL—Covered with EGG SALAD, then with BACON (broiled), and topped with shredded watercress.

SL—Covered with TOMATO slices, ANCHOVY filets, and topped with lettuce leaves.

**236   Egg Salad-Cole Slaw and Chicken-Lettuce
on White**

LL—Covered with EGG SALAD, then with COLE SLAW.

SL—Covered with sliced CHICKEN, then with lettuce leaves.

**237   Egg Salad-Green Pepper Rings and Tuna
Fish-Lettuce on Rye**

LL—Covered with EGG SALAD, then with GREEN PEPPER and topped with shredded lettuce.

SL—Covered with TUNA FISH, and topped with lettuce leaves.

**238   Egg Salad-Red Cole Slaw and Tongue-
Tomato-Lettuce on Raisin Bread**

LL—Covered with EGG SALAD, then with RED COLE SLAW.

SL—Covered with sliced TONGUE, then with TOMATO slices, and topped with lettuce leaves.

**239   Egg Salad-Tomato and Pineapple-Lettuce
on Toasted Raisin Bread**

LL—Covered with EGG SALAD, then with TOMATO slices, and topped with lettuce leaves.

SL—Covered with PINEAPPLE slice, and topped with shredded lettuce.

**240   Egg Salad-Anchovy and Tomato-Cress
on Toast**

LL—Covered with EGG SALAD, then with ANCHOVY filets, and topped with lettuce leaves.

SL—Covered with TOMATO slices, then with lettuce leaves.

241   Egg Salad-Tomato and Asparagus Tips-Lettuce on White

LL—Covered with EGG SALAD, then with TOMATO slices, and topped with lettuce leaves.

SL—Covered with ASPARAGUS TIPS, dipped in catsup, then with lettuce leaves.

242   Egg Salad-Cress and Tomato-Cream Cheese-Walnut on White

LL—Covered with EGG SALAD, then with crisp WATERCRESS.

SL—Covered with TOMATO slices, then with a mixture of CREAM CHEESE and chopped WALNUT (equal parts), and topped with lettuce leaves.

243   Egg Salad-Green Pepper Rings and Frankfurter-Lettuce on Rye

LL—Covered with EGG SALAD, then with GREEN PEPPER RINGS.

SL—Covered with skinless, sliced (lengthwise) FRANKFURTERS, spread slightly with prepared mustard, and topped with lettuce leaves.

244   Egg Salad-Olives and Swiss Cheese-Anchovy-Lettuce on Toast

LL—Covered with EGG SALAD, then with chopped black OLIVES, and topped with lettuce leaves.

SL—Covered with SWISS CHEESE, spread with ANCHOVY paste, then topped with lettuce leaves.

245   Egg Salad-Tomato and String Beans Salad-Lettuce on Rye

LL—Covered with EGG SALAD, then with TOMATO slices, and topped with lettuce leaves.

SL—Covered with STRING BEANS SALAD (French dressing), and topped with lettuce leaves.

246   Egg Salad-Anchovy and Vegetable Salad (French Dressing) on Rye

LL—Covered with EGG SALAD, then with ANCHOVY filets.

SL—Covered with VEGETABLE SALAD, topped with lettuce leaves.

**247   Egg Salad-Watercress and Pickle Relish-
           Asparagus Tips on Rye**

LL—Covered with EGG SALAD, then with crisp WATERCRESS.

SL—Covered with PICKLE RELISH, then with ASPARAGUS TIPS, and covered with lettuce leaves.

**248   Egg Salad-Tomato and Sliced Spanish
           Onion-Caviar on Toast**

LL—Covered with EGG SALAD, then with TOMATO slices and topped with lettuce leaves.

SL—Covered with sliced SPANISH ONIONS, then with CAVIAR, and topped with lettuce leaves.

**249   Egg Salad-Anchovy and Knockwurst-Cole
           Slaw-Lettuce on Rye or Pumpernickel**

LL—Covered with EGG SALAD, then with ANCHOVY filets, topped with lettuce leaves.

SL—Covered with thinly sliced KNOCKWURST sausage, spread slightly with prepared mustard, and topped with COLE SLAW and lettuce leaves.

**250   Egg (Sliced)-Shredded Lettuce (Dressed) and
           Tomato-Cress on Raisin Bread**

LL—Covered with sliced hard-cooked EGG, then topped with dressed, SHREDDED LETTUCE.

SL—Covered with TOMATO slices, then with WATERCRESS.

**251   Egg (Sliced)-Chopped Celery-Olives and
           Sardines-Lettuce on White**

LL—Covered with sliced hard-cooked EGG, then with a mixture of chopped CELERY and OLIVE meats (equal parts), topped with lettuce leaves.

SL—Covered with SARDINES, topped with lettuce leaves.

**252   Egg (Sliced)-Swiss Cheese and Ham-
Tomato-Lettuce on Toasted Rye**

LL—Covered with sliced EGG, then with SWISS CHEESE spread with prepared mustard, and topped with lettuce leaves.

SL—Covered with thinly sliced, cold, cooked HAM, then with TOMATO slices and topped with lettuce leaves.

**253   Egg (Sliced)-Cole Slaw and Tomato-Green
Pepper Rings on Toasted Rye**

LL—Covered with sliced, hard-cooked EGG, then with COLE SLAW.

SL—Covered with TOMATO slices, then with GREEN PEPPER RINGS, and topped with lettuce leaves.

**254   Egg (Sliced)-Red Cole Slaw and Potato
Salad-Lettuce on Rye**

LL—Covered with sliced, hard-cooked EGG, then covered with RED COLE SLAW.

SL—Covered with POTATO SALAD, topped with lettuce leaves.

**255   Egg (Sliced)-Ham and String Beans Salad-
Lettuce on Toast**

LL—Covered with sliced, hard-cooked EGG, then with a thin slice of HAM, topped with lettuce leaves.

SL—Covered with STRING BEANS SALAD, topped with lettuce leaves.

**256   Egg (Sliced)-Tomato-Cress and Chicken
Salad-Lettuce on White**

LL—Covered with sliced, hard-cooked EGG, then with TOMATO slices, and topped with crisp WATERCRESS.

SL—Covered with CHICKEN SALAD, then topped with lettuce leaves.

**257   Egg (Sliced)-Tomato-Cole Slaw and Ham
Salad-Lettuce on Rye**

LL—Covered with sliced, hard-cooked EGG, then with TOMATO slices, and topped with COLE SLAW.

SL—Covered with HAM SALAD, then with lettuce leaves.

258 Egg (Sliced)-Pimiento Ring and Sliced Ham-Relish-Lettuce on Rye

LL—Covered with sliced, hard-cooked EGG, then with PIMIENTO RING.

SL—Covered with thinly sliced, cold, cooked HAM, then with RELISH (any kind), and topped with lettuce leaves.

259 Egg (Sliced)-Tomato-Lettuce and Tuna Fish Salad-Lettuce on Boston Brown Bread

LL—Covered with thinly sliced, hard-cooked EGG, then with TOMATO slices, and topped with lettuce leaves.

SL—Covered with TUNA FISH SALAD, then topped with SHREDDED LETTUCE.

260 Egg (Sliced)-Bacon-Lettuce and Tomato-Cress on Toast

LL—Covered with sliced, hard-cooked EGG, then with broiled BACON, and topped with lettuce leaves.

SL—Covered with sliced TOMATOES, slightly spread with prepared mustard, then topped with WATERCRESS.

261 Egg (Sliced)-Bacon-Lettuce and Baked Beans-Lettuce on Toast

LL—Covered with sliced, hard-cooked EGG, then with broiled BACON, and topped with SHREDDED LETTUCE.

SL—Covered with BAKED BEANS (hot or cold), and topped with lettuce leaves.

262 Egg (Sliced)-Tomato-Green Pepper Rings and Salmon Salad on Toasted Rye

LL—Covered with sliced, hard-cooked EGG, then with TOMATO slices, and topped with GREEN PEPPER RINGS.

SL—Covered with SALMON SALAD, and topped with lettuce leaves.

263   Egg (Sliced)-Bacon-Olive and Potato Nut Salad-Lettuce on White

LL—Covered with sliced, hard-cooked EGG, then with broiled BACON, and topped with chopped OLIVES (any kind).

SL—Covered with POTATO NUT MEATS SALAD, and topped with lettuce leaves.

264   Egg (Sliced)-Chicken Liver and American Cheese-Cress on Toast

LL—Covered with sliced, hard-cooked EGG, then with broiled (or sauteed) CHICKEN LIVER, and topped with lettuce leaves.

SL—Covered with AMERICAN CHEESE, slightly spread with prepared mustard, and topped with WATERCRESS.

265   Egg (Sliced)-Anchovy and Tongue-Watercress on Rye

LL—Covered with sliced, hard-cooked EGG, then with ANCHOVY filets, and topped with lettuce leaves.

SL—Covered with thinly sliced, cold, cooked TONGUE, spread (slightly) with mayonnaise, and topped with WATERCRESS.

266   Egg (Sliced)-Anchovy and Tomato-Lettuce on Pumpernickel

LL—Covered with sliced, hard-cooked EGG, then with ANCHOVY filets, and topped with lettuce leaves.

SL—Covered with TOMATO slices, and topped with lettuce leaves.

267 Egg (Sliced)-Shrimp Salad and Chicken-Lettuce on White

LL—Covered with sliced, hard-cooked EGG, then with SHRIMP SALAD, and topped with lettuce leaves.

SL—Covered with sliced, cold CHICKEN, spread with mayonnaise, and topped with shredded lettuce.

268 Egg (Sliced)-Minced Ham and Nut Slaw-Cress on Toast

LL—Covered with sliced, hard-cooked EGG, then with MINCED HAM, and topped with lettuce leaves.

SL—Covered with NUT SLAW (made of equal parts of cole slaw and any kind of chopped nut meats), then topped with crisp watercress.

269 Egg (Sliced)-Bacon and Lobster Salad-Lettuce on Toast or Rye

LL—Covered with sliced, hard-cooked EGG, then with broiled BACON and topped with lettuce.

SL—Covered with LOBSTER SALAD, then topped with lettuce.

270 Egg (Sliced)-Cucumber and Banana-Cheese-Lettuce on Date Bread

LL—Covered with sliced, hard-cooked EGG, then with sliced CUCUMBER, and topped with dressed shredded cress.

SL—Covered with sliced (lengthwise) peeled BANANA, then with AMERICAN CHEESE, spread with prepared mustard, and topped with crisp lettuce leaves.

271 Ham-Swiss Cheese and Tomato-Lettuce on White

LL—Covered with thinly sliced, cooked HAM (cold), then with SWISS CHEESE, and topped with lettuce leaves.

SL—Covered with TOMATO slices, topped with lettuce leaves.

272 Ham-Cole Slaw and Tomato-Lettuce on White

LL—Covered with thinly sliced, cold, cooked HAM, then with COLE SLAW.

SL—Covered with sliced TOMATOES, spread with prepared mustard and topped with lettuce leaves.

273   Ham-Potato Salad and Tomato-Cress on Rye

LL—Covered with thinly sliced, cold, cooked HAM, then with POTATO SALAD and topped with lettuce leaves.

SL—Covered with sliced TOMATOES, spread with prepared mustard and topped with lettuce leaves.

**274   Ham-Tomato and Tongue-Swiss-Cheese-
Lettuce on Rye**

LL—Covered with thinly sliced, cold, cooked HAM, slightly spread with prepared mustard, covered with cold TONGUE, and topped with watercress.

SL—Covered with thinly sliced, cold, cooked TONGUE, then with SWISS CHEESE, and topped with lettuce leaves.

**275   Ham-Pickle Relish and Asparagus Tips-
Lettuce on Rye**

LL—Covered with thinly sliced, cold, cooked HAM, then with PICKLE RELISH, and topped with lettuce leaves.

SL—Covered with ASPARAGUS TIPS, then topped with crisp lettuce leaves.

**276   Ham-Currant Jelly and Tomato-Lettuce
on Orange Date Bread**

LL—Covered with thinly sliced, cold, cooked HAM, spread with CURRANT JELLY (or other kind of jelly), then topped with crisp lettuce leaves.

SL—Covered with TOMATO slices, slightly spread with prepared mustard, and topped with crisp lettuce leaves.

**277   Ham-Horseradish and Green Pepper Rings-
Lettuce on Boston Brown Bread**

LL—Covered with thinly sliced, cold, cooked HAM, then with prepared HORSERADISH, and topped with lettuce leaves.

SL—Covered with GREEN PEPPER RINGS, then with crisp lettuce leaves.

278 Ham-Horseradish and Potato Salad-Cress on Rye

LL—Covered with thinly sliced, cold, cooked HAM, then with HORSERADISH, and topped with lettuce leaves.

SL—Covered with POTATO SALAD, and topped with watercress.

279 Ham-Cress and Potato Salad-Lettuce on Pumpernickel

LL—Covered with thinly sliced, cold, cooked HAM, then with chopped watercress.

SL—Covered with POTATO SALAD, then with lettuce leaves.

280 Ham-American Cheese and Tomato-Anchovy-Lettuce on Toasted Rye

LL—Covered with thinly sliced, cold, cooked HAM, then spread with prepared mustard, topped with AMERICAN CHEESE, then covered with lettuce leaves.

SL—Covered with TOMATO slices, then with ANCHOVY filets, and topped with crisp lettuce leaves. (Delicious).

281 Ham-American Cheese and Tomato-Cress on Toasted Whole Wheat

LL—Covered with thinly sliced, cold, cooked HAM, spread with (slightly) horseradish, then with AMERICAN CHEESE, and topped with lettuce leaves.

SL—Covered with TOMATO slices, then generously with watercress.

282 Ham-Dill Pickle and Tomato-Lettuce on Rye

LL—Covered with thinly sliced, cold, cooked HAM, then with thinly sliced DILL PICKLES, and topped with lettuce leaves.

SL—Covered with TOMATO slices, spread with horseradish, and topped with lettuce leaves.

283 Ham-Mustard Pickle and Potato Nut Salad-Lettuce on Rye

LL—Covered with thinly sliced, cold, cooked HAM, then with thinly sliced MUSTARD PICKLE, and topped with lettuce leaves.

SL—Covered with POTATO NUT (any kind of nut meats, in equal parts) SALAD, and topped with crisp lettuce leaves.

284 Ham-Cress and Bacon-Tomato-Lettuce on Rye

LL—Covered with thinly sliced, cold, cooked HAM, then with dressed, chopped watercress.

SL—Covered with TOMATO slices, then with broiled BACON, and topped with crisp lettuce leaves.

285 Ham-Tomato and String Beans Salad-Lettuce on Whole Wheat

LL—Covered with thinly sliced, cold, cooked HAM, spread with prepared mustard, then with TOMATO slices, and topped with lettuce leaves.

SL—Covered with STRING BEANS SALAD (Mayonnaise), and topped with lettuce leaves.

286 Ham-Liederkranz Cheese and Tomato-Lettuce on Rye

LL—Covered with thinly sliced, cold, cooked HAM, then with LIEDERKRANZ CHEESE, and topped with lettuce leaves.

SL—Covered with TOMATO slices, spread with prepared horseradish, and topped with lettuce leaves.

287 Ham-Swiss Cheese and Bacon-Tomato-Lettuce on Toast

LL—Covered with thinly sliced, cold, cooked HAM, then with SWISS CHEESE, and topped with lettuce leaves.

SL—Covered with broiled BACON, then with TOMATO slices, and topped with crisp lettuce leaves.

288 Ham-Tomato-Cucumber and Egg Salad- Liverwurst-Lettuce on Toast

LL—Covered with thinly sliced, cold, cooked HAM, then with TOMATO slices, topped with thinly sliced CUCUMBER, marinated in French dressing, and covered with lettuce leaves.

SL—Covered with EGG SALAD, then with thinly sliced LIVERWURST sausage, and topped with crisp lettuce leaves.

289 Ham-Tomato and Bermuda Onion-Celery Salad-Lettuce on Toasted Rye

LL—Covered with thinly sliced, cold, cooked HAM, then with TOMATO slices, and topped with lettuce leaves.

SL—Covered with thinly sliced BERMUDA ONIONS, then with CELERY SALAD (mayonnaise), and topped with crisp lettuce leaves.

290 Ham-Potato Salad and Tomato-Pickle-Lettuce on White

LL—Covered with thinly sliced, cold, cooked HAM, then with POTATO SALAD, and covered with lettuce leaves.

SL—Covered with TOMATO slices, spread with prepared mustard and topped with crisp lettuce leaves.

291 Ham-Cream Cheese and Turkey-Cranberry-Lettuce on Toasted Whole Wheat

LL—Covered with thinly sliced, cold, cooked HAM, spread with CREAM CHEESE, and topped with watercress.

SL—Covered with sliced, cold TURKEY, spread with CRANBERRY SAUCE, and topped with lettuce leaves.

292 Ham-Tomato-Celery Green and Pepper Relish-Lettuce on Toast

LL—Covered with thinly sliced, cold, cooked HAM,

then with TOMATO slices, and topped with **chopped CELERY GREEN.**

SL—Covered first with peanut butter, then with **PEPPER RELISH,** and topped with crisp lettuce leaves.

293   Ham (Minced)-Egg Salad and Tomato-Lettuce on White

LL—Covered with MINCED HAM, mixed with prepared mustard, then with EGG SALAD, and topped with crisp lettuce leaves.

SL—Covered with TOMATO slices, topped with lettuce leaves.

294   Ham Salad-Lettuce and Tomato-Cress on Toast

LL—Covered with HAM SALAD, topped with crisp lettuce leaves.

SL—Covered with sliced TOMATOES and topped with watercress.

295   Ham Salad-Pickle Relish and Tomato-Swiss Cheese on Rye

LL—Covered with HAM SALAD, then with PICKLE RELISH (any kind) and topped with lettuce leaves.

SL—Covered with TOMATO slices, then with thinly sliced SWISS CHEESE, and topped with lettuce leaves.

296   Ham Salad-Pickle Relish and Bacon-Tomato-Lettuce on Rye

LL—Covered with HAM SALAD, then with PICKLE RELISH (any kind) and topped with lettuce leaves.

SL—Covered with broiled BACON, then with TOMATO slices, and topped with lettuce leaves.

297   Ham Salad-Pickle Relish and American Cheese-Tomato on Pumpernickel

LL—Covered with HAM SALAD, then with PICKLE RELISH (any kind) and topped with lettuce leaves.

SL—Covered with AMERICAN CHEESE, then with TOMATO slices, and topped with lettuce leaves.

**298 Ham Salad-Asparagus Tips and Tomato-Cress
on Toast**

LL—Covered with HAM SALAD, then with ASPARAGUS TIPS, and topped with lettuce leaves.

SL—Covered with TOMATO slices, spread (lightly) with prepared mustard, and topped with lettuce leaves.

299 Ham Salad-Red Cole Slaw and Tomato-Horseradish-Cress on Rye

LL—Covered with HAM SALAD, then with RED COLE SLAW.

SL—Covered with TOMATO slices, then with prepared HORSERADISH, and topped with WATERCRESS.

300 Ham Salad-Green Pepper Rings and Potato Salad-Lettuce on Rye

LL—Covered with HAM SALAD, then with GREEN PEPPER RINGS, and topped with watercress.

SL—Covered with POTATO SALAD, and topped with lettuce leaves.

**301 Ham Salad-Swiss Cheese and Apple-Lettuce
on White or Rye**

LL—Covered with HAM SALAD, then with SWISS CHEESE, slightly spread with prepared mustard, and topped with lettuce.

SL—Covered with pared, cored, APPLE slices, and topped with lettuce leaves.

**302 Ham Salad-Tomato and Potato Salad-Lettuce
on Whole Wheat**

LL—Covered with HAM SALAD, then with TOMATO slices, and topped with lettuce leaves.

SL—Covered with POTATO SALAD, then topped with shredded lettuce.

**303 Ham Salad-Cress and Tomato-Anchovy-Lettuce
on Rye**

LL—Covered with HAM SALAD, then with a generous layer of chopped watercress.

SL—Covered with TOMATO slices, then with ANCHOVY filets, and topped with lettuce leaves.

304 Ham Salad-Dill and Tomato-Cucumber-Lettuce on Rye

LL—Covered with HAM SALAD, then with thinly sliced DILL PICKLES, and topped with lettuce leaves.

SL—Covered with TOMATO slices, spread (lightly) with prepared horseradish, then with thinly sliced CUCUMBER, and topped with lettuce leaves.

305 Ham Salad-Artichoke Bottom and Tomato-Anchovy-Lettuce on White or Rye

LL—Covered with HAM SALAD, then with halved (crosswise) canned ARTICHOKE BOTTOM, and topped with lettuce leaves.

SL—Covered with TOMATO slices, spread with ANCHOVY paste, then topped with lettuce leaves.

306 Ham Salad-Raw Spinach and Bermuda Onion-Egg Salad on White

LL—Covered with HAM SALAD, then with chopped, raw SPINACH, and topped with lettuce leaves.

SL—Covered with thinly sliced BERMUDA ONION, then with EGG SALAD, and topped with lettuce leaves.

307 Ham Salad-Tomato and Spanish Onion-Caviar-Lettuce on Whole Wheat Bread

LL—Covered with HAM SALAD, then with TOMATO slices, and topped with shredded lettuce.

SL—Covered with thinly sliced SPANISH ONION, then with CAVIAR, and topped with lettuce leaves.

308 Ham Salad-Sliced Egg and Caviar-Lettuce on Toasted Rye

LL—Covered with HAM SALAD, then with sliced, hard-cooked EGG and topped with lettuce leaves.

SL—Covered with CAVIAR, then with minced onion, and topped with lettuce leaves.

309 Ham Salad-Pimiento and Navy Beans Salad-Lettuce on White

LL—Covered with HAM SALAD, then with red, canned PIMIENTO, and topped with shredded lettuce.

SL—Covered with NAVY BEANS (French dressing) SALAD, then topped with lettuce leaves.

310 Ham Salad-Gherkin and Vegetable Salad-Lettuce on Rye

LL—Covered with HAM SALAD, then with thinly sliced sweet-sour GHERKINS, and topped with lettuce leaves.

SL—Covered with VEGETABLE SALAD (mayonnaise) and topped with lettuce leaves.

311 Ham Salad-Shredded Pineapple and Tomato-Lettuce on Rye

LL—Covered with HAM SALAD, then with well-drained, canned, shredded PINEAPPLE, and topped with lettuce leaves.

SL—Covered with TOMATO slices, spread with prepared horseradish, and topped with lettuce leaves.

312 Ham Salad-Corn Salad and Chicken-Tomato-Lettuce on Toast

LL—Covered with HAM SALAD, then with canned, well-drained CORN, dressed with mayonnaise, and topped with crisp watercress.

SL—Covered with thinly sliced CHICKEN, then with TOMATO slices, and topped with lettuce leaves.

313 Ham Salad-Lettuce and Tomato-Lettuce on Toast

LL—Covered with HAM SALAD, and topped with shredded lettuce, mixed with chopped green pepper in equal parts.

SL—Covered with broiled TOMATO slices, then with watercress.

314 Ham Salad-Anchovy and Tomato-Shredded Lettuce on Rye

LL—Covered with HAM SALAD, then with ANCHOVY filets, and topped with lettuce leaves.

SL—Covered with TOMATO slices, then with shredded, dressed (French dressing) lettuce.

315 Hamburger-Cress and Egg Salad-Lettuce on Toast

LL—Covered with pancake-like, panned HAMBURGER, and topped with chopped watercress.

SL—Covered with EGG SALAD (mayonnaise), and topped with lettuce leaves.

316 Hamburger-Chopped Bacon and Swiss Cheese-Lettuce on Toast

LL—Covered with pancake-like, broiled HAMBURGER, then with chopped BACON, and topped with lettuce leaves.

SL—Covered with thinly sliced SWISS CHEESE, spread with prepared mustard, and topped with lettuce leaves.

317 Hamburger-Mustard Pickles and Pineapple-Lettuce on Rye

LL—Covered with pancake-like, panned HAMBURGER, then with MUSTARD PICKLES, and topped with watercress.

SL—Covered with a slice of canned PINEAPPLE (well-drained) and topped with lettuce leaves.

318 Hamburger-Shredded Pineapple and Tomato-Lettuce on Raisin Bread

LL—Covered with pancake-like, broiled HAMBURGER, then with canned, well-drained, shredded PINEAPPLE, and topped with lettuce leaves.

SL—Covered with TOMATO slices, spread with prepared mustard and topped with lettuce leaves.

319 Hamburger-Bermuda Onion and Ham-Dill-Lettuce on Rye

LL—Covered with pancake-like, panned HAMBURGER,

then with thinly sliced BERMUDA ONION and topped with watercress.

SL—Covered with thinly sliced, cold, cooked HAM, then with thinly sliced DILL PICKLES, and topped with lettuce leaves.

320 Hamburger-Sauerkraut and Tomato-Bacon-Lettuce on Pumpernickel or Rye

LL—Covered with pancake-like, broiled HAMBURGER, then with well-drained, canned SAUERKRAUT.

SL—Covered with TOMATO slices, chopped BACON and topped with lettuce leaves.

321 Hamburger-Tomato and Curried Egg-Lettuce on Toast

LL—Covered with pancake-like, panned HAMBURGER, then with TOMATO slices, and topped with watercress.

SL—Covered with CURRIED EGG (cold), and topped with lettuce leaves.

322 Hamburger-Sliced Egg and Orange Marmalade-Lettuce on Nut Bread

LL—Covered with pancake-like, broiled HAMBURGER, then with sliced, hard-cooked EGG, and topped with watercress.

SL—Covered with ORANGE MARMALADE, then topped with shredded lettuce.

323 Hamburger-Lettuce and Chicken Salad-Lettuce on White

LL—Covered with pancake-like, broiled HAMBURGER, and topped with shredded lettuce.

SL—Covered with CHICKEN SALAD, topped with lettuce leaves.

324 Hamburger-Liederkranz Cheese and Tongue-Tomato-Lettuce on Pumpernickel or Rye

LL—Covered with pancake-like, broiled HAMBURGER, then with LIEDERKRANZ CHEESE, and topped with lettuce leaves.

SL—Covered with TONGUE slices, then with TOMATO slices, and covered with lettuce leaves.

325 Hamburger-Cress and Cream Cheese-Raspberry Jam-Lettuce on Raisin Bread

LL—Covered with pancake-like, broiled HAMBURGER, then with dressed, chopped watercress (French dressing and well-drained.)

SL—Covered with CREAM CHEESE, mixed in equal parts with RASPBERRY JAM, and topped with lettuce leaves.

326 Hamburger-Bean Salad and Orange Marmalade-Nut-Cress on Orange Date Bread

LL—Covered with pancake-like, panned HAMBURGER, then with BEAN SALAD, and topped with lettuce leaves.

SL—Covered with ORANGE MARMALADE mixed, in equal parts with chopped NUT MEATS (any kind) and topped with crisp watercress.

327 Hamburger-Broiled Ham and Potato Salad-Nut-Lettuce on Rye

LL—Covered with pancake-like, panned HAMBURGER, then with a thin slice of HAM, spread with prepared mustard, and topped with lettuce leaves.

SL—Covered with POTATO SALAD, mixed with equal parts of chopped NUT MEATS, and topped with lettuce leaves.

328 Hamburger-Smothered Onions and American Cheese-Lettuce on Boston Brown Bread

LL—Covered with pancake-like, panned HAMBURGER, then with cold, smothered ONIONS (well-drained from any fat) and topped with lettuce leaves.

SL—Covered with a thin slice of AMERICAN CHEESE, spread with prepared horseradish, and topped with lettuce leaves.

329 Hamburger-Fried Tomato and String Beans Salad-Lettuce on Toast

LL—Covered with pancake-like, panned HAMBURGER,

then with hot, fried TOMATOES, and topped with lettuce leaves.

SL—Covered with STRING BEANS SALAD, and topped with lettuce leaves.

330 Hamburger-Dill and Bermuda Onion-Tomato-Lettuce on Rye

LL—Covered with pancake-like, broiled HAMBURGER, then with thinly sliced DILL PICKLES, and topped with chopped watercress.

SL—Covered with thinly sliced BERMUDA ONION, then with TOMATO slices, and topped with lettuce leaves.

331 Hamburger-Horseradish and American Cheese-Lettuce on Toast

LL—Covered with pancake-like, fried HAMBURGER, then spread with prepared horseradish, and topped with lettuce leaves.

SL—Covered with thinly sliced AMERICAN CHEESE, spread with prepared mustard, and topped with lettuce leaves.

332 Hamburger-Pickle Relish and Cucumber Salad-Lettuce on Rye

LL—Covered with pancake-like, broiled HAMBURGER, then with PICKLE RELISH, and topped with shredded lettuce.

SL—Covered with well-drained CUCUMBER SALAD (mayonnaise), and topped with lettuce leaves.

333 Hamburger-American Cheese and Bacon-Lettuce on Whole Wheat

LL—Covered with pancake-like, panned HAMBURGER, then topped with AMERICAN CHEESE, and covered with lettuce leaves.

SL—Covered with broiled BACON, spread with prepared mustard and topped with lettuce leaves.

334 Herring Filets-Cucumber Salad and American Cheese-Cress on Whole Wheat Bread

LL—Covered with well-drained, canned HERRING FILETS, then with CUCUMBER SALAD (French dressing), and topped with lettuce leaves.

SL—Covered with AMERICAN CHEESE, and topped with watercress.

335 Herring Salad-Lettuce and Swiss Cheese-Lettuce on Rye

LL—Covered with HERRING SALAD (made of equal parts of minced herring filets and potato salad, and a little French dressing).

SL—Covered with thinly sliced SWISS CHEESE, spread (lightly) with prepared mustard, and topped with lettuce leaves.

336 Herring Filets-Tomato and Green Pepper Rings-Dill-Cress on Rye

LL—Covered with well-drained, canned, HERRING FILETS, then with TOMATO slices, spread with ANCHOVY PASTE (lightly) and topped with lettuce leaves.

SL—Covered with GREEN PEPPER RINGS, then with thinly sliced DILL PICKLES, and topped with crisp watercress.

337 Herring Filets-Red Cole Slaw and Bermuda Onion-Pimiento on Rye

LL—Covered with well-drained, canned HERRING FILETS, then with RED COLE SLAW, and topped with lettuce leaves.

SL—Covered with thinly sliced BERMUDA ONION, then with PIMIENTO slice, and topped with lettuce leaves.

338 Herring Filets-Tomato and Crab Meat Salad on Pumpernickel

LL—Covered with well-drained, canned HERRING FILETS, then with TOMATO slices, and topped with lettuce leaves.

SL—Covered with CRAB MEAT SALAD, and topped with lettuce leaves.

339   Herring Filets-Bermuda Onion and Tomato-Cress on Rye

LL—Covered with well-drained, sponged, canned HERRING FILETS, then with thinly sliced BERMUDA ONIONS and topped with lettuce leaves.

SL—Covered with TOMATO slices, spread with prepared mustard and topped with crisp watercress.

340   Herring Filets-Potato Salad and Tomato-Lettuce on Toasted Pumpernickel

LL—Covered with well-drained, sponged, canned HERRING FILETS, then with POTATO SALAD, and topped with lettuce leaves.

SL—Covered with TOMATO slices, spread with mixed, prepared mustard and horseradish, in equal parts, and topped with lettuce leaves.

341   Herring Filets-String Beans Salad and Tomato-Cress on Toasted Rye

LL—Covered with well-drained, sponged, canned HERRING FILETS, then with well-drained STRING BEANS SALAD, and topped with crisp lettuce leaves.

SL—Covered with TOMATO slices, then with crisp watercress.

342   Herring Filets-Tomato and Salmon Salad-Lettuce on Toasted Rye

LL—Covered with well-drained, sponged, canned HERRING FILETS, then with TOMATO slices, and topped with crisp lettuce leaves.

SL—Covered with SALMON SALAD (French dressing and well-drained), and topped with lettuce leaves.

343   Herring Filets-Dill and Tuna Fish Salad-Lettuce on Rye

LL—Covered with well-drained, sponged, canned HERRING FILETS, then with thinly sliced DILL PICKLES, and topped with lettuce leaves.

SL—Covered with TUNA FISH SALAD (French dressing, and well-drained) and topped with crisp, green lettuce leaves.

344 Honey-Almond Paste and Cream Cheese-Lettuce on Orange Bread

LL—Covered with strained HONEY, then with ALMOND PASTE, and topped with lettuce leaves.

SL—Covered with CREAM CHEESE, and topped with lettuce.

345 Honey-Walnut Meats and Toasted Marshmallow-Shredded Coconut on Orange Bread

LL—Covered with strained HONEY, then sprinkled (generously) with chopped WALNUT MEATS, and topped with lettuce leaves.

SL—Covered with toasted MARSHMALLOWS, then with shredded COCONUT.

346 Honey-Raisin and Cream Cheese-Nut Meats-Lettuce on Raisin Bread

LL—Covered with strained HONEY, then sprinkled with puffed (parboiled) seedless RAISINS, and covered with lettuce leaves.

SL—Covered with CREAM CHEESE, generously sprinkled with chopped NUT MEATS, and topped with lettuce leaves.

347 Honey-Pineapple and Persimmon-Lettuce on Orange Biscuit

LL—Covered with strained HONEY, then sprinkled (generously) with well-drained, shredded, canned PINEAPPLE, and topped with lettuce leaves.

SL—Covered with the pulp of ripe PERSIMMON, mixed with a few drops of lemon juice, and topped with shredded lettuce.

348 Honey-Banana and Cream Cheese-Jelly-Lettuce on Raisin Bread

LL—Covered with strained HONEY, then with skinned, sliced BANANA, and topped with shredded lettuce.

SL—Covered with CREAM CHEESE, mixed with equal parts of CURRANT or any other kind of jelly, and topped with shredded lettuce.

349   Honey-Liederkranz Cheese and Tomato-Lettuce on Rye

LL—Covered with strained HONEY, then with LIEDERKRANZ CHEESE, and topped with chopped watercress.

SL—Covered with TOMATO slices, then with shredded lettuce, the sandwich should be cut in four, from corner to corner, and held with toothpick.

350   Honey-Turkey and Cream Cheese-Olive-Nut-Lettuce on Boston Brown Bread

LL—Covered with strained HONEY, then with thinly sliced cold TURKEY, and topped with lettuce leaves.

SL—Covered with a mixture of CREAM CHEESE, OLIVE MEATS, NUT MEATS, in equal parts, and well blended, and topped with crisp, green lettuce leaves.

351   Honey-Ham-Cress and Cranberry Sauce-Nut Meats-Lettuce on Nut Bread

LL—Covered with strained HONEY, then with sliced HAM, and topped with crisp watercress.

SL—Covered with CRANBERRY SAUCE, mixed with equal parts of NUT MEATS, and topped with lettuce leaves.

352   Jellied Chicken and Tomato-Lettuce on White

LL—Covered with JELLIED CHICKEN, and topped with lettuce leaves.

SL—Covered with TOMATO slices, spread with mixed horseradish and prepared mustard, in equal parts, and topped with lettuce leaves.

353   Jellied Crab Meat and String Beans Salad-Lettuce on White

LL—Covered with JELLIED CRAB MEAT, then with shredded lettuce.

SL—Covered with STRING BEANS SALAD, and topped with lettuce leaves.

354   Jellied Minced Ham-Apple and Cucumber-Cole Slaw on Toasted Rye

LL—Covered with JELLIED MINCED HAM, then with pared, cored COOKING APPLE, and topped with lettuce leaves.

SL—Covered with sliced CUCUMBER, covered with COLE SLAW, and topped with lettuce leaves.

355   Jellied Lobster and Tomato-Cress on Toast

LL—Covered with JELLIED LOBSTER, then topped with crisp watercress.

SL—Covered with TOMATO slices, spread with prepared mustard and covered with crisp watercress.

356   Jellied Ox Tongue-Cress and Swiss Cheese-Lettuce on Whole Wheat Bread

LL—Covered with JELLIED OX TONGUE, and topped with watercress.

SL—Covered with SWISS CHEESE, spread with prepared mustard, and topped with crisp, green lettuce leaves.

357   Jellied Turkey-Cress and Bacon-Tomato-Lettuce on White

LL—Covered with JELLIED TURKEY, then topped with watercress.

SL—Covered with broiled BACON, then with TOMATO slices, spread with prepared mustard, and topped with lettuce.

358   Jellied Veal-Cress and Tomato-Lettuce on White

LL—Covered with JELLIED VEAL, then topped with watercress.

SL—Covered with TOMATO slices, spread with prepared horseradish, and topped with lettuce leaves.

**359 Jelly- (any kind) Banana and Peanut Butter-
Lettuce on Orange Bread**

LL—Covered with JELLY (using any kind desired), then with peeled, sliced BANANA, and topped with chopped watercress.

SL—Covered with PEANUT BUTTER, and topped with dressed, shredded lettuce.

**360 Liverwurst-Pickle Relish and Bacon-Tomato-
Lettuce on Toasted Rye**

LL—Covered with sliced LIVERWURST SAUSAGE, then with PICKLE RELISH, and topped with lettuce leaves.

SL—Covered with broiled (cold) BACON, then with TOMATO slices, and topped with lettuce leaves.

**361 Liverwurst-Tomato and American Cheese-
Lettuce on Toasted Rye**

LL—Covered with thin slice (or slices) of LIVERWURST, then with TOMATO slices, spread with prepared mustard, and topped with lettuce leaves.

SL—Covered with AMERICAN CHEESE, spread with prepared horseradish, and topped with lettuce leaves.

**362 Liverwurst-Cole Slaw and American Cheese-
Lettuce on Toasted Rye**

LL—Covered with LIVERWURST, then with COLE SLAW, and topped with lettuce leaves.

SL—Covered with AMERICAN CHEESE, spread with prepared mustard, and topped with lettuce leaves.

**363 Liverwurst-Bacon and Anchovy-Tomato-
Lettuce on Toasted Whole Wheat**

LL—Covered with LIVERWURST, then with broiled BACON, and topped with lettuce leaves.

SL—Covered with sponged ANCHOVY FILETS, then with TOMATO slices, and topped with lettuce leaves.

**364 Liverwurst-Cress and Cream Cheese-Nut-
Lettuce on Toast**

LL—Covered with LIVERWURST, then with chopped watercress.

SL—Covered with CREAM CHEESE, mixed in equal parts with chopped NUT MEATS (any kind), and topped with lettuce.

365 Liverwurst-Cucumber and Tongue-Lettuce on Rye

LL—Covered with LIVERWURST, spread with horseradish, then topped with sliced, pared CUCUMBER.

SL—Covered with sliced TONGUE, spread with prepared mustard, then topped with lettuce leaves.

366 Liverwurst-Bermuda Onion and Corned Beef-Lettuce on Toasted Roll

LL—Covered with LIVERWURST, spread with prepared mustard, then with thinly sliced BERMUDA ONION, and topped with shredded lettuce.

SL—Covered with CORNED BEEF, spread with a mixture of prepared horseradish and mustard, in equal parts, then topped with lettuce leaves.

367 Liverwurst-Fruit-Nut Slaw and Ham-Tomato-Lettuce on Rye

LL—Covered with LIVERWURST, then with a mixture of assorted, canned FRUITS (well-drained, and chopped) with equal parts of NUT MEATS (any kind), and topped with lettuce.

SL—Covered with thinly sliced, cold, cooked HAM, then with TOMATO slices and topped with lettuce leaves.

368 Liverwurst-Potato Salad and Swiss Cheese-Lettuce on Rye

LL—Covered with LIVERWURST, then with POTATO SALAD, and topped with lettuce leaves.

SL—Covered with SWISS CHEESE, spread with prepared mustard, and topped with lettuce leaves.

369 Liverwurst-Red Cole Slaw and Roquefort-Lettuce on Whole Wheat Bread

LL—Covered with LIVERWURST, then with RED COLE SLAW, and topped with lettuce leaves.

SL—Covered with ROQUEFORT CHEESE, then with crisp lettuce leaves.

370   Liverwurst-Sliced Egg and Tomato-Grated Onion-Lettuce on Rye

LL—Covered with LIVERWURST, then with sliced, hard-cooked EGG, and topped with lettuce leaves.

SL—Covered with TOMATO slices, then with grated ONION, mixed with prepared mustard, and topped with lettuce leaves.

371   Lobster-Tartar Sauce and Fried Mushrooms-Lettuce on White

LL—Covered with coarsely chopped LOBSTER, mixed with TARTAR SAUCE and capers, and topped with lettuce leaves.

SL—Covered with fried MUSHROOMS, and topped with lettuce.

372   Lobster Salad-Nut Meats and Sliced Pineapple-Lettuce on Toast

LL—Covered with LOBSTER SALAD mixed in equal parts with NUT MEATS and mayonnaise, then topped with lettuce leaves.

SL—Covered with a slice of canned, well-drained PINEAPPLE, and topped with lettuce leaves.

373   Lobster-Catsup-Dill and Tomato-Nut-Olive-Lettuce on Rye

LL—Covered with sliced LOBSTER, then spread with TOMATO CATSUP, and topped with lettuce leaves.

SL—Covered with TOMATO slices, spread with a mixture of NUT and OLIVE MEATS, mixed with mayonnaise, and topped with lettuce leaves.

374   Lobster-Chopped Cress and Tomato-Green Pepper Rings on Whole Wheat Bread

LL—Covered with chopped LOBSTER, mixed with mayonnaise and chopped cress (in equal parts), and topped with lettuce.

SL—Covered with TOMATO slices, spread with prepared mustard and covered with GREEN PEPPER RINGS, then with lettuce.

375   Mushroom-Chopped Bacon and Tomato-Lettuce on Toast

LL—Covered with sliced, fried MUSHROOMS, mixed (in equal parts) with chopped, broiled BACON, and topped with lettuce leaves.

SL—Covered with TOMATO slices, spread with prepared horseradish (well-drained) and topped with lettuce leaves.

376   Mushroom-Crab Meat and Tuna Fish Salad-Lettuce on Toast

LL—Covered with fried, sliced MUSHROOMS, mixed with flaked CRAB MEAT, and topped with crisp watercress.

SL—Covered with TUNA FISH SALAD, and topped with lettuce leaves.

377   Mushroom-Chopped Egg and Pineapple-Lettuce on Toasted Raisin Bread

LL—Covered with fried, sliced MUSHROOMS, mixed with chopped, hard-cooked EGG, and topped with chopped watercress.

SL—Covered with well-drained PINEAPPLE slice, and topped with lettuce leaves.

378   Mushroom-Fried Onion and Tomato-Bacon-Lettuce on Toasted Rye

LL—Covered with sliced, fried MUSHROOMS, mixed with fried ONIONS (well-drained) and topped with shredded lettuce.

SL—Covered wiht TOMATO slices, broiled BACON, and topped with lettuce leaves.

379   Mushroom-Chicken and Bacon-Sliced Tomato-Lettuce on Toast

LL—Covered with broiled MUSHROOMS (well drained), then with sliced CHICKEN, and topped with watercress.

SL—Covered with broiled BACON, then with TOMATO slices, and topped with lettuce leaves.

380 Nut Meats-Olive Meats-Whipped Cream and Pineapple-Lettuce on Fig Bread

LL—Covered with a mixture of NUT and OLIVE MEATS, mixed with WHIPPED CREAM, and topped with shredded lettuce.

SL—Covered with a well-drained PINEAPPLE slice (canned) and topped with lettuce leaves.

381 Nut Meats-Olive Meats-Green Pepper and American Cheese on Raisin Bread

LL—Covered with a mixture of chopped NUT MEATS, OLIVE MEATS and chopped GREEN PEPPER (in equal parts) mixed with mayonnaise, and topped with lettuce.

SL—Covered with AMERICAN CHEESE, spread with prepared mustard, and topped with lettuce leaves.

382 Nut Meats-Chopped Liver and Apple Celery Salad-Lettuce on Rye

LL—Covered with chopped NUT MEATS mixed with cooked, chopped BEEF (or any other liver) LIVER, and topped with watercress.

SL—Covered with APPLE (chopped) and CELERY (chopped) SALAD mixed with mayonnaise, and topped with lettuce leaves.

383 Nut Meats-Cranberry Jelly and Turkey-Lettuce on Toasted French Bread

LL—Covered with chopped NUT MEATS, mixed with CRANBERRY JELLY in equal parts, and topped with chopped watercress.

SL—Covered with sliced, cold, cooked TURKEY, spread with horseradish (prepared) and topped with lettuce leaves.

384 Nut Meats-Fig-Cress and Veal-Dill-Lettuce on Orange Peel Bread

LL—Covered with chopped NUT MEATS and chopped,

dried FIGS, mixed with mayonnaise, and topped with crisp watercress.

SL—Covered with sliced VEAL, then with thinly sliced DILL PICKLE, and topped with lettuce leaves.

385   Onion Salad-Cucumber and Tomato-Chopped Bacon-Lettuce on Rye

LL—Covered with ONION SALAD (French dressing and well-drained) then with sliced CUCUMBERS, and topped with crisp, green lettuce.

SL—Covered with TOMATO slices, then with chopped, broiled BACON and topped with lettuce leaves.

386   Onion-Baked Beans and Frankfurter-Pickle-Lettuce on Boston Brown Bread

LL—Covered with thinly sliced BERMUDA ONION (raw), then with BAKED BEANS, and topped with lettuce leaves.

SL—Covered with skinned, sliced (lengthwise) FRANKFURTER SAUSAGE, then with thinly sliced sweet-sour PICKLE, and topped with lettuce leaves.

387   Onion-Dill-Cucumber-Radish and Ham-Lettuce on Rye

LL—Covered with thinly sliced BERMUDA ONION, spread with prepared mustard, then with thinly sliced DILL PICKLES, and again with sliced RED RADISHES, topped with mayonnaise dressed shredded lettuce.

SL—Covered with sliced, cooked HAM, spread with prepared mustard, and topped with lettuce leaves.

388   Onion-Pineapple-Lettuce and Tomato-Bacon-Lettuce on Toast

LL—Covered with thinly sliced BERMUDA ONION, dipped in French dressing and well-drained, then covered with a slice of canned PINEAPPLE (well-drained), and topped with lettuce leaves.

SL—Covered with TOMATO slices, spread with prepared mustard then with chopped, broiled BACON, and topped with lettuce.

389 Onion-Nut Meats and Liver-Bacon-Lettuce on Toast

LL—Covered with creamed ONIONS (the sauce should be rather thick), mixed with chopped WALNUT MEATS, and topped with shredded lettuce.

SL—Covered with a slice of LIVER (any kind), broiled very rare, covered with broiled BACON, and topped with lettuce.

390 Peanut Butter-Bacon and Tomato-Lettuce on Toasted Rye

LL—Covered with PEANUT BUTTER, then with fried BACON (well-drained), and topped with lettuce leaves.

SL—Covered with TOMATO slices, spread with prepared horseradish, and topped with lettuce leaves.

391 Peanut Butter-Pineapple and American Cheese-Lettuce on Corn Bread

LL—Covered with PEANUT BUTTER, then with PINEAPPLE slice, and topped with shredded lettuce mixed with mayonnaise.

SL—Covered with AMERICAN CHEESE, spread with mustard, then topped with lettuce leaves.

392 Peanut Butter-Chopped Cress and Cream Cheese-Celery on Honey Bread

LL—Covered with PEANUT BUTTER, then with chopped watercress.

SL—Covered with CREAM CHEESE, mixed with chopped CELERY, and topped with lettuce leaves.

393 Peanut Butter-Olive-Nut Meats and Tomato-Bacon-Cress on Pumpernickel

LL—Covered with PEANUT BUTTER, then with a mixture (in equal parts) of OLIVE and NUT MEATS, and topped with lettuce.

SL—Covered with TOMATO slices, then with chopped BACON, and shredded watercress.

394 Peanut Butter-Chopped Walnut and Pot Cheese-Chives on Rye or White

LL—Covered with PEANUT BUTTER, then with chopped WALNUTS, and topped with shredded lettuce mixed with mayonnaise.

SL—Covered with rather dry POT CHEESE, mixed with minced CHIVES (parsley may be substituted), and topped with lettuce leaves.

395 Peanut Butter-Orange Marmalade and Swiss Cheese-Cress on Date Nut Bread

LL—Covered with PEANUT BUTTER, then with ORANGE MARMALADE, and topped with minced watercress.

SL—Covered with SWISS CHEESE, spread with prepared mustard, and topped with minced watercress.

396 Peanut Butter-Olive Meats and American Cheese-Dill on Toasted Rye

LL—Covered with PEANUT BUTTER, then with chopped, pitted BLACK OLIVES, and topped with shredded lettuce.

SL—Covered with AMERICAN CHEESE, spread with horseradish, and topped with thinly sliced DILL PICKLE, then with shredded lettuce.

397 Peanut Butter-Lettuce-Green Pepper and Tongue-Swiss Cheese-Lettuce on Raisin Bread

LL—Covered with PEANUT BUTTER, then with a mixture of shredded lettuce and chopped GREEN PEPPER, mixed with mayonnaise.

SL—Covered with cold, sliced, cooked TONGUE, then with SWISS CHEESE, spread (lightly) with prepared mustard, and topped with lettuce leaves.

398 Peanut Butter-Red Cole Slaw and Pineapple-Lettuce on Nut Bread

LL—Covered with PEANUT BUTTER, then with RED COLE SLAW, and topped with crisp watercress.

SL—Covered with PINEAPPLE, and topped with lettuce leaves.

399   Peanut Butter-Sliced Orange and Celery Green-Lettuce on Cheese Biscuit

LL—Covered with PEANUT BUTTER, then with peeled, sliced, seedless ORANGES, and topped with chopped watercress.

SL—Covered with chopped CELERY GREEN, mixed with mayonnaise and topped with lettuce leaves.

400   Peanut Butter-Pineapple and Liederkranz-Lettuce on Orange Rye Bread

LL—Covered with PEANUT BUTTER, then with shredded (well-drained) PINEAPPLE, and topped with lettuce leaves.

SL—Covered with LIEDERKRANZ CHEESE, then sprinkled with caraway seeds, then topped with lettuce leaves.

401   Peanut Butter-Celery Stalks and Tongue-Raisins-Tomato-Lettuce on Rye

LL—Covered with PEANUT BUTTER, then with small CELERY STALKS.

SL—Covered with sliced TONGUE, spread with chopped RAISINS, then with TOMATO slices, and topped with lettuce leaves.

402   Peanut Butter-Cream Cheese-Poppy Seeds and Pineapple-Cress on Date Bread

LL—Covered with PEANUT BUTTER, then with softened CREAM CHEESE, and sprinkled with POPPY SEEDS, and topped with lettuce leaves.

SL—Covered with shredded PINEAPPLE (well-drained), then topped with crisp watercress.

403   Peanut Butter-Orange Marmalade and American Cheese-Cress on Nut Bread

LL—Covered with PEANUT BUTTER, then with ORANGE MARMALADE, and topped with lettuce leaves.

SL—Covered with AMERICAN CHEESE, spread with prepared horseradish, and topped with chopped watercress.

404 Peanut Butter-Prunes and Pork-Sweet Pickle-Lettuce on Nut Bread

LL—Covered with PEANUT BUTTER, then with cooked, pitted PRUNES, and topped with lettuce leaves.

SL—Covered with sliced, well-cooked PORK, then with chopped SWEET PICKLE, and topped with lettuce leaves.

405 Peanut Butter-Sardine and Potato Salad-Lettuce on Rye

LL—Covered with PEANUT BUTTER, then with boneless SARDINE and topped with shredded lettuce.

SL—Covered with POTATO SALAD, then with lettuce leaves.

406 Peanut Butter-Banana and Orange Marmalade-Lettuce on Baking Powder Biscuit

LL—Covered with PEANUT BUTTER, then with sliced BANANAS, and topped with lettuce leaves.

SL—Covered with ORANGE MARMALADE, then with shredded lettuce.

407 Peanut Butter-Cranberry and Crushed Bacon-Banana-Cress on Baking Powder Biscuit

LL—Covered with PEANUT BUTTER, then with whole CRANBERRY SAUCE, and topped with lettuce leaves.

SL—Covered with crushed, broiled BACON, then with sliced BANANAS, and topped with crisp watercress.

408 Peanut Butter-Ham and Egg Salad-Lettuce on Toasted Rye

LL—Covered with PEANUT BUTTER, then with HAM, and topped with shredded lettuce.

SL—Covered with EGG SALAD, then with lettuce leaves.

409 Peanut Butter-Dates-Nut and Tomato-Onion-Lettuce on Orange Bread

LL—Covered with PEANUT BUTTER, then with a mixture of pitted, chopped DATES, and NUT MEATS (in equal parts) mixed with mayonnaise, and topped with lettuce leaves.

SL—Covered with TOMATO slices, topped with thinly sliced BERMUDA ONION, spread with horseradish, and covered with lettuce leaves.

410 Peanut Butter-Pimiento-Green Pepper Rings and Swiss Cheese-Lettuce on White

LL—Covered with PEANUT BUTTER, then with a whole slice of canned PIMIENTO (well-drained), and again with GREEN PEPPER RINGS, and topped with lettuce leaves.

SL—Covered with SWISS CHEESE, spread with prepared mustard and topped with lettuce leaves.

411 Pork-Apple Sauce and Cabbage Salad-Lettuce on Rye

LL—Covered with thinly sliced, well-cooked ROAST PORK, then with rather thick APPLE SAUCE, and covered with shredded lettuce.

SL—Covered with CABBAGE SALAD (mayonnaise) and topped with lettuce leaves.

412 Pork-Dill-Green Pepper Rings and American Cheese-Cress on Pumpernickel

LL—Covered with cold, roasted PORK (well-done), then with GREEN PEPPER RINGS, and topped with lettuce leaves.

SL—Covered with AMERICAN CHEESE, spread with prepared mustard, and topped with crisp watercress.

413 Pork-Swiss Cheese and Potato Salad-Lettuce on Rye

LL—Covered with well-cooked ROAST PORK, then with a thin slice of SWISS CHEESE, and topped with lettuce leaves.

SL—Covered with POTATO SALAD, then with crisp lettuce leaves.

414   Pork-Baked Beans and Tomato-Lettuce on White or Rye

LL—Covered with sliced, well-done ROAST PORK, then with cold BAKED BEANS, and topped with lettuce leaves.

SL—Covered with TOMATO slices, spread with prepared mustard and topped with lettuce leaves.

415   Pork-Apple-Cress and String Beans Salad-Lettuce on Rye

LL—Covered with a slice or two of ROAST PORK (cold), then with thin slices of pared, cored, raw APPLE, and topped with chopped watercress.

SL—Covered with STRING BEANS SALAD (French dressing) and topped with lettuce leaves.

416   Pork-Pineapple-Cress and Tomato-Dill-Lettuce on Nut Bread

LL—Covered with sliced, cold, ROAST PORK, then with a PINEAPPLE slice (well-drained) and topped with crisp watercress.

SL—Covered with TOMATO slices, then with thinly sliced DILL PICKLE, and topped with lettuce leaves.

417   Pork-Orange-Onion and Tomato-Lettuce on Rye

LL—Covered with sliced, cold PORK, then with ORANGE slices (peel removed), and topped with thinly sliced BERMUDA ONION, and topped with lettuce leaves.

SL—Covered with TOMATO slices, spread with a mixture of prepared mustard and horseradish (in equal parts), and topped with lettuce leaves.

418   Salmon Salad-Cress and Asparagus Tips-Tomato-Lettuce on Toast

LL—Covered with SALMON SALAD, then with crisp watercress.

SL—Covered with ASPARAGUS TIPS, then with TOMATO slices, spread with prepared mustard, and topped with lettuce.

419 Salmon Salad-Nut Meats and Sliced Egg-Lettuce on Toast

LL—Covered with SALMON SALAD, then topped with chopped NUT MEATS, and topped with lettuce leaves.

SL—Covered with sliced, hard-cooked EGG, then with shredded lettuce, mixed with mayonnaise mixed with a little catsup.

420 Salmon Salad-Raw Spinach and Tomato-Bacon-Lettuce on White

LL—Covered with SALMON SALAD, then with chopped, raw SPINACH, and topped with lettuce leaves.

SL—Covered with TOMATO slices, spread with mustard, then with broiled BACON, and topped with lettuce leaves.

421 Salmon-Sweet Relish and Egg-Apple-Lettuce on White or Rye

LL—Covered with a mixture (paste) of canned SALMON and ground SWEET RELISH, then topped with shredded lettuce.

SL—Covered with sliced, hard-cooked EGG, then thinly sliced, pared, cored APPLE, and topped with lettuce leaves.

422 Salmon-Walnuts-Olives-Celery and American Cheese-Cress on Toast

LL—Covered with a mixture (paste) made of equal parts each of SALMON, chopped WALNUTS, OLIVE MEATS, and minced CELERY, mixed with a little seasoned heavy cream, and topped with shredded watercress.

SL—Covered with AMERICAN CHEESE, topped with watercress.

**423 Sardine-Lettuce and Tomato-Anchovy-Lettuce
on White**

LL—Covered with boned SARDINES, then with shredded lettuce, mixed with French dressing.

SL—Covered with TOMATO slices, then with 2 ANCHOVY filets, and topped with lettuce leaves.

424 Sardine-Sliced Egg and Bermuda Onion-Pineapple-Cress on Rye

LL—Covered with boneless SARDINES, then with a little catsup, and covered with sliced, hard-cooked EGG, then topped with lettuce leaves.

SL—Covered with thinly sliced BERMUDA ONION, then with a slice of canned PINEAPPLE, and topped with crisp watercress.

**425 Sardine-Scrambled Egg and Tomato-Lettuce
on Whole Wheat**

LL—Covered with boneless SARDINES, then with cold, scrambled EGG, and topped with lettuce leaves.

SL—Covered with TOMATO slices, then spread with prepared mustard, and topped with lettuce leaves.

**426 Sardine-Cress and Caraway Cheese-Lettuce
on Nut Bread**

LL—Covered with boneless SARDINES, then with chopped watercress mixed with mayonnaise.

SL—Covered with CARAWAY CREAM CHEESE (cream cheese mixed with caraway seeds), and topped with lettuce leaves.

**427 Sardine-Tomato and Baked Beans-Lettuce
on Whole Wheat Bread**

LL—Covered with boneless SARDINES, then with TOMATO slices spread with prepared horseradish, and topped with lettuce leaves.

SL—Covered with BAKED BEANS (cold), highly seasoned, and topped with lettuce leaves.

428 Sardine-Tomato and Cucumber-Onion-Lettuce on Rye

LL—Covered with boneless SARDINES, then with TOMATO slices spread with a little mayonnaise, and topped with lettuce leaves.

SL—Covered with sliced CUCUMBER (dressed with French dressing) then with a thin slice of BERMUDA ONION, and topped with lettuce leaves.

429 Sardine-Onion-Cress and Swiss Cheese-Dill-Lettuce on Whole Wheat Bread

LL—Covered with boneless SARDINES, then with chopped ONION, and topped with crisp watercress.

SL—Covered with SWISS CHEESE, spread with prepared mustard, then with thinly sliced DILL PICKLE, and topped with lettuce leaves.

430 Sardine-American Cheese and Shrimp Salad-Lettuce on Toasted Whole Wheat Bread

LL—Covered with boneless SARDINES, then with AMERICAN CHEESE, and topped with shredded lettuce.

SL—Covered with SHRIMP SALAD (mayonnaise) and topped with lettuce leaves.

431 Sardine-Tomato and Onion-Caviar-Lettuce on Rye

LL—Covered with boneless SARDINES, then with TOMATO slices, and topped with lettuce leaves.

SL—Covered with thinly sliced BERMUDA ONION, then with CAVIAR, and topped with lettuce leaves.

432 Sardine-Egg and Scallions-Radishes-Lettuce on White or Rye

LL—Covered with boneless SARDINES, then with sliced, hard-cooked EGG, sprinkled or rather dotted here and there with catsup mayonnaise, and topped with lettuce leaves.

SL—Covered with SCALLIONS, then with sliced RADISHES, and topped with lettuce leaves.

**433   Sardine-Olive-Lettuce and Tomato-Cucumber-
          Lettuce on White or Rye**

LL—Covered with boneless SARDINES, then with chopped, pitted OLIVE MEATS, and topped with shredded lettuce.

SL—Covered with sliced TOMATOES, then spread with mayonnaise, and topped with CUCUMBER (sliced thin), and covered with lettuce leaves.

**434   Sardine-Broiled Onion and Swiss Cheese-
          Lettuce on Whole Wheat Bread**

LL—Covered with boneless SARDINES, then with a thin slice of broiled BERMUDA ONION, and topped with lettuce leaves.

SL—Covered with SWISS CHEESE, topped with prepared horseradish, and covered with lettuce leaves.

**435   Sardine-Bacon and Tomato-Sweet Relish-
          Lettuce on Rye**

LL—Covered with boneless SARDINES, then with broiled BACON, and topped with lettuce leaves.

SL—Covered with TOMATO slices, then with chopped (well-drained) SWEET RELISH and topped with lettuce leaves.

**436   Sardine-Anchovy-Cress and Bacon-Cucumber-
          Tomato-Cress on Rye**

LL—Covered first with a thin film of ANCHOVY paste, then with boneless SARDINES, and topped with watercress.

SL—C o v e r e d with chopped BACON, then with chopped, pared CUCUMBER, mixed with a little mayonnaise, then with TOMATO slices, and topped with crisp watercress.

**437   Sardine-Nut Meats and Crab Meat Salad-
          Lettuce on Orange Bread**

LL—Covered with boneless SARDINES, then with chopped NUT MEATS mixed with a little mayonnaise, then topped with lettuce leaves.

SL—Covered with CRAB MEAT salad, then topped with lettuce leaves.

438 Sardine (Mashed)-Green Pepper-Pimiento and Salami-Lettuce on White

LL—Covered with a mixture of SARDINE, mashed, and chopped GREEN PEPPER and PIMIENTO (in equal parts), blended with tomato catsup, then topped with lettuce leaves.

SL—Covered with sliced SALAMI, spread with prepared mustard, then topped with lettuce leaves.

439 Sardine (Mashed)-Nut Meats-Olive and Salami-Tomato-Lettuce on Rye

LL—Covered with a paste made of equal parts of SARDINE, NUT MEATS and chopped BLACK OLIVES, then blended with a little mayonnaise, and topped with lettuce leaves.

SL—Covered with SALAMI, spread with horseradish, then with TOMATO slices, and topped with lettuce leaves.

440 Sardine (Mashed)-Pineapple and Tomato-Anchovy-Lettuce on Whole Wheat Bread

LL—Covered with mashed SARDINES, then with shredded, well-drained PINEAPPLE, and topped with lettuce leaves.

SL—Covered with TOMATO slices, spread with ANCHOVY paste, and topped with lettuce leaves.

441 Sardine (Mashed)-Horseradish and Shrimp Salad-Lettuce on Rye

LL—Covered with mashed SARDINES, mixed with equal parts of prepared horseradish, and topped with shredded lettuce, mixed with chopped pimiento.

SL—Covered with SHRIMP SALAD, then topped with lettuce.

442 Shrimp Salad-Shredded Pineapple and Tomato-Lettuce on Toast

LL—Covered with SHRIMP SALAD, mixed in equal

parts with well-drained, canned, shredded PINEAPPLE, and topped with lettuce leaves.

SL—Covered with TOMATO slices, spread with tomato catsup, and topped with lettuce leaves.

443   Shrimp Salad-Nut Meats and American Cheese-Lettuce on Rye

LL—Covered with SHRIMP SALAD, mixed with chopped NUT MEATS, and topped with lettuce leaves.

SL—Covered with AMERICAN CHEESE, spread with well-drained prepared horseradish, and topped with lettuce leaves.

444   Shrimp Salad-Cucumber and Tongue-Green Pepper-Lettuce on Boston Brown Bread

LL—Covered with SHRIMP SALAD, mixed with cubed CUCUMBER, and topped with chopped watercress.

SL—Covered with sliced, cold, cooked TONGUE, then with GREEN PEPPER RINGS, and topped with lettuce.

445   Shrimp Salad-Tomato and Veal-Green Pepper Rings-Lettuce on Pumpernickel

LL—Covered with SHRIMP SALAD, then with TOMATO slices, and topped with lettuce leaves.

SL—Covered with cooked, cold, sliced VEAL, spread with thinly sliced DILL PICKLE, spread with prepared mustard, and covered with GREEN PEPPER RINGS, and topped with lettuce leaves.

446   Tomato Salad-Bacon and American Cheese-Cole Slaw-Cress on Rye

LL—Covered with TOMATO SALAD, then with broiled or fried BACON, and topped with lettuce leaves.

SL—Covered with AMERICAN CHEESE, then with COLE SLAW, and topped with crisp watercress.

447   Tuna-Tomato-Dill and Anchovy-Red Cole Slaw-Lettuce on Rye

LL—Covered with sliced TUNA FISH, then with TOMATO, spread (thinly) with prepared mustard, then with thinly sliced DILL PICKLES, and topped with lettuce leaves.

SL—Covered with ANCHOVY filets, then with RED COLE SLAW, and topped with lettuce leaves.

448 Tuna Salad-Pimiento and Sliced Egg-Green Pepper Rings on Rye

LL—Covered with TUNA FISH SALAD (mayonnaise), then with chopped red PIMIENTO, and topped with chopped watercress.

SL—Covered with sliced, hard-cooked EGG, dotted here and there with well-drained prepared horseradish, and with GREEN PEPPER RINGS, then topped with lettuce leaves.

449 Vegetable Salad-Cress and Asparagus Tips-Red Cabbage on White or Rye

LL—Covered with VEGETABLE SALAD (mayonnaise or French dressing may be used), topped with chopped watercress.

SL—Covered with ASPARAGUS TIPS, then with shredded (fine) RED CABBAGE, mixed with mayonnaise or catsup.

SANDWICHES

450   COLOR EFFECTS IN SANDWICHES

Because dainty sandwiches are suitable for service with both beverages soft and hard, as well as dairy beverages, sandwich making today is a tailor-made art. No longer does the old-fashioned, hunger-satisfying slab of bread and meat or cheese pass muster at the modern cafeteria, lunch-counter and restaurant. The sandwich-maker who would please his patrons with tantalizing tidbits of bread, seasoned spreads and what not, must be a past-master at *tailoring* his sandwiches. And although mass production is sometimes called for, monotony is absolutely taboo. The modern sandwich-maker must make ultra-sandwiches, yet reasonably priced. Not only must his technique be perfect but he must have a flair for the unusual for filling and decoration.

Color contrasts are possible by making use of a dark and light bread in the same sandwich, by the familiar method of placing one white slice of bread on top of another dark slice, such as whole wheat, rye or pumpernickel, to say nothing of Boston brown bread.

The next important step in sandwich making is the choice of a foundation spread for the bread. It is no more accepted, nor desired in sandwich-making to spread plain uncreamed butter on the bread. After the preliminary duties are attended to the major part of sandwich-making is centered in the selection of filling. Today, the filling may be placed between two, or even three slices of the same or different breads, or it may grace the top of a single slice (open sandwiches), placing a buttered slice next to it. Two different fillings may be used if they go together.

The filling for a sandwich, like the trimming on a dress, should be outstanding enough to express the personality of the sandwich-maker, and should also, like the proper dress, be suitable to the customer.

Sandwiches, because they offer so many opportunities for variety and fit beautifully into the lighter menu, are delightful, in any kind of season.

451 SUGGESTIONS FOR SEASONED AND COMPOUNDED BUTTERS FOR SANDWICHES

Besides plain butter, the sandwich-maker who wants to create a reputation and do a volume of business—hence free advertisement by word of mouth—may have on hand or prepares on the spur of the demand seasoned or compounded butters for spread which will keep a long time in refrigerator or ice boxes, for spread, then cover the butter with the called for filling or fillings, which ranges from the original roast beef to peanuts.

For these butters proceed as follows:

To each half cup (¼ lb.) of butter, add the following.

452   Almond Butter

Work in 2 tablespoons blanched, ground almonds and a few drops of lemon juice.

453   American Cheese Butter

Work in 2 tablespoons grated American cheese, and add a few drops of Worcestershire sauce.

454   Anchovy Butter

Work in a few drops of lemon juice, the size of a pea (more or less, according to taste) of anchovy paste, and ½ teaspoon finely minced parsley.

455   Apple Sauce Butter

Work in 2 tablespoons rather firm apple sauce and 1 tablespoon ground nut meats.

456   Apricot Butter

Work in 2 tablespoons of cooked, sieved apricot (rather firm) and a few drops of lemon juice.

457   Catsup Butter

Work in 3 tablespoons catsup and 1 teaspoon grated onion.

458   Caviar Butter

Work in 1 tablespoon well-drained caviar, a few drops lemon juice, and ½ teaspoon grated onion.

459   Chili Butter

Work in 3 tablespoons chili sauce and a few drops lemon juice.

460   Chive Butter

Work in 2 tablespoons finely minced chives and 1 teaspoon grated onion.

461   Chutney Butter

Work in 1 generous tablespoon of ground mustard chutney, and a few drops of Tabasco sauce.

462 Cress Butter

Work in 3 tablespoons of finely minced watercress.

463 Egg Yolk Butter

Work in 1 hard sieved, cooked egg yolk, a few drops of onion juice and 1 tablespoon finely minced parsley.

464 Green Pepper Butter

Work in 3 tablespoons grated, well-drained or squeezed between dry towels green pepper and a few drops of lemon juice.

465 Garlic Butter

Blanch in a few drops of water or vinegar, a small clove of garlic. Remove, dry and mash. Work in to the butter.

466 Herring Butter

Work in 1 tablespoon of ground, free from any bone smoked herring and a few drops of lemon juice.

467 Honey Butter

Work in 1 tablespoon of strained honey and a few drops each of Tabasco sauce and lemon.

468 Horseradish Butter

Work in 2 tablespoons, well drained or squeezed prepared horseradish and 1 tablespoon finely minced chives.

469 Jam Butter

Work in 2 tablespoons of any kind of jam and a few drops of lemon juice.

470 Jelly Butter

Work in 2 tablespoons of any kind of jelly, and a few drops of lemon juice. (You may add 1 tablespoon of any kind of ground nut meats, if desired.)

471   Lemon Butter

Add to teaspoons lemon juice to creamed butter, and ½ teaspoon grated lemon rind.

472   Liverwurst Butter

Work in 3 tablespoons of mashed liverwurst sausage and a few drops of lemon juice, or 1 teaspoon grated onion.

473   Lobster Butter

Work in ½ cup (equal parts) cooked, ground lobster, and a few drops of lemon juice.

474   Molasses Butter

Work in 1 teaspoon molasses and ¼ teaspoon grated lemon or orange rind.

475   Mustard Butter

Work in 2 (more or less) teaspoons prepared mustard and a few drops of lemon juice.

476   Nut Butter

Work in 2 tablespoons of any kind of ground nut meats, and ¼ teaspoon grated orange rind.

477   Olive Pimiento Butter

Run in 2 chopped pimientos and ¼ cup of chopped, stuffed olives and let stand in refrigerator over night to mellow before using.

478   Orange Butter

Add 2 teaspoons of orange juice and ½ teaspoon grated orange rind.

479   Peanut Butter

Use plain or mixed with equal parts of sweet, creamed butter and peanut butter.

480   Parsley Butter

Work in 2 tablespoons finely minced parsley and a few drops of Tabasco sauce, or Worcestershire sauce.

481   Paprika Butter

Work in 1 tablespoon of paprika and a few drops of onion juice.

482   Pimiento Butter

Work in 2 tablespoons of finely chopped, then well-squeezed between towels of red pimiento.

483   Pineapple-Ginger Butter

Work in 2 tablespoons of canned, crushed and squeezed between towls of pineapple mixed with a few grains of ginger powder.

484   Potted Meat Butter

Work in any kind of canned, or tubed potted meat paste, as, deviled ham, tongue, chicken, etc., using 2 generous tablespoons and a few drops of onion and lemon juices.

485   Prune Butter

Work in 2 tablespoons cooked, sieved, rather stiff or firm prune pulp, and add ½ teaspoon grated lemon rind.

486   Roquefort Cheese Butter

Work in 2 generous tablespoons of Roquefort cheese mashed with a few drops of Worcestershire sauce.

487   Shrimp Butter

Work in 1½ generous tablespoons of cooked, canned or fresh shrimps, ground or pounded to a paste, and a few drops each of lemon and onion juices.

488   Sardine Butter

Work in ¼ cup boned, skinned, and thoroughly drained canned sardines, with ½ teaspoon each of onion, and lemon juice and a few drops of Tabasco sauce.

489 **Salmon Butter**

Using fresh cooked, or smoked salmon. Work in 2 tablespoons of ground or pounded to a paste of salmon, a few drops of lemon juice and Worcestershire sauce.

490 **Tarragon Butter**

Work in 2 or 3 leaves of fresh tarragon, chopped very fine, and a few drops of tarragon vinegar.

491 **Vegetable Butter**

Work in any kind of cold, cooked, ground green vegetables, a few drops of lemon juice, 1 teaspoon of grated onion, and a few drops of Tabasco sauce.

SANDWICH FILLINGS

492 **SANDWICH FILLINGS**

Gone are the days when food for the purposes of cooling was hung in wells. Gone, too, are the days when milk cans flanked the brook's edge. Correct temperatures, measuring and the right proportions mean perfect results. Today good judgment is needed to build a well-balanced meal; a good palate is necessary to season the foods to a perfect taste, and any good cook book will supply the necessary inspiration and information for infinite variety in the menu, especially in sandwich-making. Cooks sometimes think that the spices and seasonings called for in a recipe can be omitted and still get good results. They think that the eighth of a teaspoon of pepper and of other spices will never be missed, or that it won't make any difference in the finished product. There could be no greater mistake. It is just as fatal as omitting some of the other basic ingredients. The sandwich may look all right without these little seasoners, but it won't have the perfection of tastiness which it should have.

Certain seasonings lift up certain foods, but in using them the cook must be careful not to over-season, but rather to obtain a delicious blend which will bring out the flavor of the predominant ingredient in the dish, even in a sandwich, and add that elusive aroma so subtle that even the epicure hesitates to name it. Food properly seasoned is an art in itself, so season your sandwiches as you would your other dishes.

There are dozens of spices which American cooks seldom use because they do not know how to taste for them when preparing foods. But wonders can be worked with them by a cook who has the imagination to try them and who also knows how to taste. Palates would probably be more pleased at mealtime, and profits would be increased at the end of the day, too, if many cooks gave up the idea of *cooking by ear* or by guess and by gosh, and cook by taste.

493   SANDWICH FILLING SUGGESTIONS

For folks who count calories, for ladies who wish to keep slim, for afternoon callers or patrons, for the small purse, and for profit to their makers.

NOTE.—

(a) All hot sandwich fillings may be served upon hot waffles or freshly made toast, according to demand.

(b) For every filling the kind of bread is indicated, but is not a rigid prescription.

(c) All the following fillings may be used for canapes, or appetizers, when garnished accordingly.

(d) Sandwiches, filled with the following fillings, **may** be left open, covered, halved or quartered from corner to corner.

(e) The proper garnishing is left to the imagination of the maker.

(f) It is understood that covered sandwich, be they halved from the middle, or triangular, or quartered, should be covered with either lettuce leaves or watercress or shredded red or green cabbage before being covered.

(g) The basis of these fillings is either plain bread, nut bread, fruit bread, rye bread, or any other kind of bread, according to demand.

(h) All and everyone of the following fillings, have been tested, and may be prepared in advance when put into a jar, covered with a buttered paper and kept in a refrigerator or ice box.

(i) 1 cup of filling will fill about 7 full-sized sandwiches.

1¼ cups of filling will fill about 9 full full-sized sandwiches.

1½ cups of filling will fill about 11 full-sized sandwiches.

2 cups of filling will fill about 15 full-sized sandwiches.

(j) Bread or toast used for spreading these fillings may be spread with either plain butter or either one of the Seasoned and Compounded Butters for Sandwiches.

494   Anchovy and Parmesan Cheese Filling

Serve on toast. Makes 1 generous cup.

To 10 tablespoons of freshly grated Parmesan cheese, add 1 tablespoon of anchovy paste (or more, if desired sharp). Beat well with a little mayonnaise, and spread between freshly made toast.

495   American Cheese and Nut Filling

Serve on rye bread. Makes 1 generous cup.

To 10 tablespoons grated fresh American cheese, add ¼ cup coarsely chopped nut meats, moisten with a little mayonnaise.

496   Apple and Peanut Butter Filling

Serve on whole wheat bread. Makes 1 generous cup.

To 10 tablespoons of pared, cored, finely chopped eating apple, add quickly 1 teaspoon of lemon juice, and mix with softened peanut butter, using about 4 tablespoons, mixed with a little mayonnaise.

497 **Apricot Filling I**
Any kind of bread. Makes 2 generous cups.

Soak ½ scant lb. dried apricots in cold water for 4 hours after washing them well. Drain and chop. Add ¾ cup granulated sugar, shredded rind of ½ large orange; ½ cup chopped seedless raisins, and ½ cup chopped nut meats. Cook over a gentle fire for an hour, stirring occasionally. Cool and chill. Spread between slices of buttered bread.

498 **Apricot Filling II**
Serve on hot toast. Makes 1 cup.

Boil 1 cup soaked dried apricots, uncovered with 2 cups water and ½ cup granulated sugar for 10 minutes, cover and simmer 15 to 20 minutes. Remove from the fire and sieve. Then add 3 tablespoons of ground blanched almonds, cool. Store. When needed heat the required amount and spread between toast. Cut in four from corner to corner.

499 **Avocado Filling**
Serve on rye. Makes 1 cup.

Put 1 cup of avocado pulp through ricer. Add 2 teaspoons lemon juice, ½ teaspoon onion juice and 1 scant teaspoon salt. Stir until smooth.

500 **Baked Beans Horseradish Filling**
Serve on toast. Makes 1 generous cup.

Put 1 generous cup of cold baked beans into a sieve and rub through. Add 3 tablespoons of drained, prepared horseradish, a few drops Worcestershire sauce, and blend well.

501 **Crab Meat Filling**
Serve either on toast or any kind of bread.
Makes 2½ cups.

Lobster, shrimp, and tuna fish or salmon as well as chicken, veal or pork may be prepared in the same way.

Mix all the ingredients, after boning whenever necessary, as well as flaking well. Add ½ cup finely minced celery, 1½ tablespoons grated onion, and ½ scant cup mayonnaise. Blend well. Keep in refrigerator until wanted.

502   Carrot Filling
Serve on graham bread. Makes 1½ cups.

To 1 cup grated raw carrots add 5 tablespoons mayonnaise, 1 scant teaspoon salt, a few grains of pepper, ½ cup broken nut meats, 1 tablespoon lemon juice and a few drops of Worcestershire sauce. Blend well. Store in ice box until wanted.

503   Chicken Filling I
Serve on toast. Makes 1¼ cups.

Put ½ cup cold cooked chicken, 3 olives, ½ green pepper, 2 hard-cooked eggs through food chopper, add 1½ teaspoons chili sauce, 3 tablespoons mayonnaise or more to moisten and a few drops of Worcestershire sauce. Mix well. Store until wanted.

504   Chicken Filling II
Serve on buttered graham bread. Makes 1½ cups.

Chop very fine enough cold cooked chicken so as to obtain 1 cup. Do not grind. Combine with ½ cup of finely chopped nut meats, and enough well seasoned mayonnaise to which has been added 1 tablespoon of prepared mustard. Store in refrigerator until wanted.

505   Cottage Cheese Filling
Serve on any desired bread. Makes 1½ cups.

Sieve 1 cup cottage cheese, add 2 tablespoons each of minced chives, grated onion and minced parsley, and 2 tablespoons minced green olives. Season to taste with salt and white pepper. Store in ice box. Does not keep very long.

506   Cream Cheese Filling
Proceed as indicated for No. 505 above, Cottage Cheese Filling, substituting cream cheese for cottage cheese.

507   Cream Cheese and Banana Filling

Serve on canned or fresh date and nut bread or Boston brown bread. Makes 1 cup.

Sieve 1 large banana with 1 teaspoon lemon juice to prevent darkening with a package of cream cheese also sieved once then with the banana pulp, and a few grains of salt to taste. Does not keep long.

508   Cream Cheese, Chives and Pineapple Filling

Serve on any kind of bread, especially raisin bread. Makes 2 cups.

Cream 2 package of cream cheese with 2 or 3 tablespoons of finely minced chives and 2 tablespoons of mayonnaise, and blend with 1 cup of well-drained, canned crushed pineapple. Keeps well.

509   Cream Cheese and Honey Filling

Serve on rye, Boston brown bread or graham bread. Makes 1 cup.

Blend 1 package of cream cheese with ½ cup of strained honey and 3 tablespoons of blanched ground almonds. Keeps 3 or 4 weeks.

510   Creamed Hamburger Filling

Serve on toast, spread with peanut butter. (Hot)— Makes 1 cup.

Cook 1 tablespoon minced onion in 1 tablespoon of fat, then add ½ lb. hamburger steak, chopped coarsely, season with salt and pepper and 1½ tablespoon minced parsley. Cook 10 minutes, stirring well, then add enough thick white sauce to moisten. Keeps well.

511   Dried Beef and American Cheese Filling

Serve on white bread. Makes 1 cup.

Blend ½ cup of ground dried beef and ½ cup ground American cheese, moisten with a little catsup and a few grains of dry mustard. Keeps very long.

512   **Dried Beef Filling Country Style**

Serve on white bread. Makes 1¼ cups.

Put ¼ lb. dried beef and ¼ lb. American cheese through food chopper. Mix with 1/3 cup canned tomato sauce and cook in double boiler till heated and well blended. Remove from heat, add I well-beaten whole egg and a little pepper, no salt at all. Cool. Keeps several weeks.

513   **Dried Beef and Horseradish Filling**

Serve on pumpernickel or Boston brown bread. Makes 1 cup.

Blend together 1 cup ground dried beef, enough French dressing to moisten and 4 tablespoons of well-drained, prepared horseradish. Keeps 3 weeks.

514   **Dried Beef and Peanut Butter Filling**

Serve on plain or toasted bread. Makes 2 cups.

Mix 1 cup peanut butter and ½ cup, scalded, drained, then ground dried beef, then add ½ scant cup of chili sauce, and 2 tablespoons minced parsley. Keeps several weeks.

515   **Egg Mayonnaise Filling**

Serve on graham bread. Makes 1 cup.

Finely chop the whites of 6 hard-cooked eggs. Press the hard-cooked yolks through potato ricer. Mix yolks and whites, season to taste with salt and paprika and moisten with mayonnaise or cream salad dressing. Keeps 1 week.

516   **Far East Filling**

Serve on plain bread. Makes 1½ cups.

Cook 2 large white onions, minced, ½ green pepper, minced, and ½ cup minced celery (you may add one small clove of garlic, minced, if desired) in 3 tablespoons of fat, slowly until vegetables soften, stirring, frequently. Season with salt, pepper and ½ teaspoon of curry powder (more curry may be added, if desired). Drain the oil from 2 large cans of sardines (boneless) and mince, or rather mash them thoroughly. Add sardines to cooked vegetables with ¼ cup minced sweet pickles, 8 pitted green olives minced fine and 6 hard-cooked eggs, minced. Moisten with mayonnaise, a little lemon juice and a few drops of Tabasco sauce. Blend well and keep in a jar, in refrigerator until wanted. Keeps months.

517   Fig and Date Filling
Serve on thin slices of nut bread. Makes 2 cups.

Put enough dried figs and enough dates through food chopper so as to obtain 1 cup of each kind. Add just enough cold water, to barely cover and cook to form a paste. Add then I teaspoon lemon juice. Cool. Keeps several weeks.

518   Fish Roe Mayonnaise Filling
Serve on peanut buttered toast. Makes 1 serving.

Grain about 2½ to 3 tablespoons of any kind of cooked or smoked fish roe, moisten with mayonnaise and add 1 teaspoon of grated onion. Do not keep.

519   Fluffy Peanut Butter Filling
Serve on raisin bread. Makes 1½ cups.

Mix together ¾ cup peanut butter and ¼ cup lemon juice, 2 tablespoons sugar, salt to taste and eonugh evaporated milk to make of spreading consistency. Whip until very light and fluffy. Keeps 1 week.

520   Ginger and Date Filling
Serve on graham bread spread with peanut butter. Makes 1½ cups.

Mix ½ cup finely chopped dates, ½ cup chopped (not ground) walnuts and a generous ¼ cup of chopped preserved ginger. Moisten with a little lemon juice or ginger syrup. Blend thoroughly. Keeps 2 or 3 weeks.

521   Ham and Jelly Filling

Serve on white or whole wheat bread. Makes 2 cups.

Cream ½ cup of butter and blend with 1 cup finely chopped or ground ham and ½ cup currant jelly, mixed with 1 teaspoon of paprika. Keeps 2 weeks.

522   Ham and Mayonnaise Filling

Serve on white or Boston brown bread. Makes 1 cup.

Blend 1¼ cups ground ham, 6 tablespoons mayonnaise, 3 tablespoons finely chopped chutney, 1½ tablespoons chutney syrup. Mix well. Keeps weeks.

523   Ham and Raw Vegetable Filling

Serve on rye bread. Makes 1 cup.

Grind or grate raw vegetables, as carrots, onions, green pepper etc. enough to make ½ generous cup. Add and blend well ½ cup ground ham, and moisten with mayonnaise, salt and pepper to taste. Keeps a few days.

524   Ham and Walnut Meats Filling

Serve on white bread. Makes 1½ cups.

Combine and blend thoroughly 1 cup ground ham, ½ cup chopped walnut meats, 1 tablespoon prepared mustard and 4 tablespoons of mayonnaise or fresh cream. Season to taste with salt, pepper and a few drops of Tabasco sauce. Keeps several weeks.

525   Ham, Giblets and Egg Filling

Serve on buttered toast. Makes 1 cup.

Clean and cook giblets from one chicken in boiling salted water until tender. Drain, put through food chopper with ½ scant cup of cooked ham and 1 hard-cooked egg Blend with 2 tablespoons of mayonnaise or cream, 1 tablespoon grated onion, ½ teaspoon Worcestershire sauce, 1 tablespoon tomato catsup and salt and pepper to taste. Keeps 3 or 4 weeks.

526   Honey Nut Filling
Serve on buttered whole wheat. Makes 1 cup.

Combine and mix thoroughly ½ cup each of strained honey and chopped nut meats. Keeps indefinitely.

527   Liver and Bacon Filling
Serve on rye or Boston brown bread. Makes 1 cup.

Broil 8 slices of bacon. Broil ¼ lb. beef liver, just enough to remove the rawness. Grind bacon and liver and season to taste, add 1 tablespoon grated onion, 1 tablespoon minced chives, salt and pepper and 1 teaspoon Worcestershire sauce. Blend thoroughly. Keeps 1 week.

528   Liver and Egg Filling
Serve on any kind of bread. Makes 2 cups.

Brown ½ lb. beef liver in butter 3 minutes. Remove the skin and tubes, cut into small pieces and grind, adding the fat from the pan, add 1 tablespoon grated onion, 1 tablespoon minced parsley, 1 tablespoon minced green pepper, a few drops of Tabasco sauce, ½ teaspoon Worcestershire sauce, salt and pepper to taste and 2 hard-cooked eggs, also put through food chopper. Add 2 tablespoons of mayonnaise, and blend thoroughly. Store in a small jar in the refrigerator until wanted. Keeps 1 week, or even two.

529   Liver and Olive Filling
Serve on toast or upon hot waffles. Makes 2 cups.

Cook 1 lb. beef liver 5 minutes in boiling salted water. Drain, remove the skin and tubes and grind with 1 cup of ripe olives. Moisten with mayonnaise, season to taste with salt and pepper. Blend thoroughly. Store in jar and keep in refrigerator. Keeps 2 weeks.

530   Midinette Filling
Serve on toast. Makes 2 cups.

Combine and mix thoroughly ½ cup strained honey, ½ cup peanut butter, 1 cake of sieved cream cheese, ¼ cup ground seedless raisins, and ¼ cup ground nut meats. Season with salt and pepper to taste. Store in a jar, and keep in refrigerator until wanted. Keeps 2 weeks or longer.

531   Orange and Grapefruit Marmalade, Cottage Cheese Filling
Serve on toast, spread with peanut butter. Makes 2 cups.

Combine and mix well ½ cup each of orange and grapefruit marmalade, and 1 cup well-drained cottage cheese, sieved. Season with salt and pepper, and 1 tablespoon of minced chives or parsley. Store in a jar, and keep in refrigerator until wanted. Keeps 1 long week.

532   Peach and Nut Meats Filling
Serve on buttered white bread. Makes 2 cups.

Combine 1 cup of fresh or canned peach pulp, ½ cup of ground nut meats, and ½ cup of ground chicken, add 1 teaspoon ground cinnamon and season with salt and pepper to taste. Keeps 1 week.

533   Prunes and Nut Filling
Serve on buttered white bread. Makes 2 cups

Sieve enough cooked prunes so as to obtain 1 cup of pulp. Add 1 tablespoon lemon juice and 1 cup of ground nut meats. Season to taste with salt and pepper. Store in a jar and keep in refrigerator. Keeps 3 weeks.

534   Roquefort Cheese Filling
Serve on any kind of bread. Makes 1 cup.

Combine and mix to a paste ½ cup Roquefort cheese, ½ cup cream cheese, and 1 generous teaspoon Worcestershire sauce, season with salt and pepper to taste. Keep sealed in refrigerator. Keeps 2 weeks.

535   Roquefort Cheese and Cress Filling
Serve on rye or Boston brown bread. Makes 1 cup.

Cream enough Roquefort cheese so as to make 1 cup, with ¼ cup of finely chopped watercress, add 1 teaspoon Worcestershire sauce, and season with salt and paprika. Store in a jar, and keep in a refrigerator. Keeps 2 weeks.

536 Roquefort Cheese and Nut Filling
Serve on rye or Boston brown bread. Makes 1 cup.

Cream enough Roquefort cheese so as to make ¾ cup of paste, adding a little mayonnaise to ease the creaming, add ¼ cup finely chopped nut meats (not ground). Season with a few drops of Tabasco, 1 teaspoon Worcestershire sauce, blend well. Place in a jar and keep in refrigerator until wanted. Keeps 2 weeks.

537 Roquefort Cheese and Camembert and Ham Filling
A very delicious mixture, a favorite of Park Avenue, served on pumpernickel or Boston brown bread. Makes 1½ cups.

Cream together ½ cup each of camembert and Roquefort cheese, with ½ cup of ground walnut meats. Add 1 teaspoon each of Worcestershire sauce and tomato catsup and season with salt, pepper and a few grains of curry powder. Blend thoroughly. Put in a jar, and keep in refrigerator until wanted. Keeps months.

538 Spicy Ham Filling
Serve on any kind of bread. Makes 2 cups.

Combine 1 cup ground cooked ham, 1/3 cup finely chopped or ground pickles, 1/3 cup ground ripe olives, 1 tablespoon each of finely minced parsley, onion and red pimiento, 2 teaspoons brown sugar, ½ teaspoon dry mustard and salt and pepper to taste. Moisten with mayonnaise. Put in a jar, and keep in refrigerator until wanted. Keeps 2 weeks.

539 Spicy American Cheese Filling
Serve on any kind of bread. Makes 5 cups.

Place 2 cups of strained canned tomatoes (juice and pulp forced through a fine sieve), salt and pepper to taste, ½ teaspoon dry mustard, in a double boiler and cook until mixture boils violently, add 2 tablespoons of tapioca and continue boiling, stirring constantly, until tapioca is done, about 5 minutes. Add then 2 generous cups of grated American cheese, and stir until melted. Remove from hot water, add 1 cup of ground dried beef, and ½ teaspoon Worcestershire sauce. Blend well. Cool. It will thicken as it cools. Place in a jar, keep in refrigerator until wanted. Keeps 1 month.

540   Spicy Savory Filling

Serve on any kind of bread. Makes 1 generous cup.

Mix together ½ cup minced cooked bacon, ½ cup peanut butter, 2 teaspoons of Worcestershire sauce, a few grains of curry powder and enough tomato catsup to moisten. Does not keep long.

541   Spicy Shrimp and Caper Mayonnaise Filling

Serve on any kind of bread. Makes 3½ cups.

Use 2 cups of cooked fresh or canned shrimp. Mince 2 cups of shrimps very fine, and combine with ¾ cup finely chopped celery, 1/3 cup chopped capers, ¼ cup of mayonnaise, and 1 teaspoon each of curry powder and Worcestershire sauce. Blend thoroughly. Keep in a jar or several jars, in refrigerator until wanted. Keeps 2 or 3 weeks.

542   Spicy Sardine Filling

Serve on plain bread or on toast. Makes about 3 cups.

Drain 2 cans sardines (boneless) and mash. There should be 1 scant cup, and combine with 2 slices of bread, soaked in milk (hot), using about ¼ cup, squeeze and add to sardine paste with 2 hard-cooked eggs, ground, black pepper and salt to taste, 2 or 3 tablespoons vinegar, 1 teaspoon sugar, 3 tablespoons minced parsley, 3 tablespoons minced green pepper, ½ clove garlic, mashed, 1 tablespoon Worcestershire sauce, 1 teaspoon curry powder, ¼ cup ground ripe olives, a few drops of Tabasco sauce, and 4 tablespoons of butter. Mash and beat, adding a little tomato catsup to ease mashing. Pack in a jar and keep until wanted. Keeps 3 to 4 weeks.

543   Spicy Salmon Filling

Serve on plain bread or on toast. Makes about 3 cups.

Proceed as indicated for No. 542, Spicy Sardine Filling, substituting salmon for sardines.

544   Texas Filling

Serve on white bread or buns. Makes 2 cups.

Put through food chopper any kind of scraps of leftover meats, there should be 2½ cups. Add 2 tablespoons grated onions. Combine with ½ cup of tomato juice, season highly with salt, a pinch of cayenne pepper and 1 teaspoon of chili powder. Cook until mixture is thoroughly blended and reaches the boiling point, stirring constantly. Cool or serve hot. Keeps well 2 or 3 weeks.

545   Tongue and Ham Filling

Serve on graham or white bread. Makes 2 cups.

Grind enough cold cooked tongue, and cold cooked ham, so as to obtain 1 cup of each, and blend thoroughly with paprika, salt and pepper to taste. Add also 1 teaspoon of prepared mustard and 1 teaspoon Worcestershire sauce, 1 tablespoon of grated onion and 1 tablespoon of minced parsley. Moisten with either catsup or mayonnaise or both, pack in a jar, and keep in refrigerator until wanted. Keeps 2 weeks.

546   Tongue and Horseradish Filling

Serve on any kind of bread. Makes 2 cups.

To 1 cup of ground cooked tongue, add 3 tablespoons prepared drained horseradish, 3 tablespoons chili sauce, 2 tablespoons minced green pepper, 2 tablespoons minced onions and ½ cup chopped ripe olives. Season with 1 tablespoon Worcestershire sauce, salt and pepper to taste and moisten with mayonnaise. Pack in a jar, and keep in refrigerator until wanted. Keeps 2 weeks.

547   Tongue And Pork Filling

Serve on buttered raisin bread. Makes 2 cups.

Combine 1 cup cold, cooked, ground tongue and 1 cup of cold, cooked, ground pork, and add 3 tablespoons each of green pepper, parsley and grated onion. Season with salt and pepper, and 1 teaspoon of Worcestershire sauce. Blend thoroughly, moistening with catsup mayonnaise. Pack in jar and keep in refrigerator until wanted. Keeps 2 weeks.

TOASTS

548   TOASTS

From just the ordinary, everyday ingredients that you have always on hand, you are able to almost magically produce a truly delightful toast. For breakfast, luncheon or supper, vary the toast, feature as many toasts as possible, as this will pay great dividends. Feature toast made with almost any kind of bread. Use fresh bread for a moist center. Day-old bread can be used for this type of toast. For dry crisp toast, bread should be at least one day old and must be browned slowly. For the crisp, shiny finish desirable for grilled sandwiches, butter one side of bread before toasting and put sandwiches together buttered side out. To make crisp, dry Melba toast, cut bread as thin as possible and brown slowly in a slow oven.

549   Baltimore Toast

A variation of French Toast. (Serves 6)

Mix 2 well-beaten eggs, ½ cup sugar, 2 cups of milk, a few grains salt to taste, and 2 teaspoons ground cinnamon. Dip 12 slices (2 to a portion) of bread in this mixture, then in flour. Fry in hot deep fat. Serve hot with jelly or jam.

550   Banana Cinnamon Toast

Cut crusts from bread slices. Spread lightly with butter. Toast. Cut in two triangles. Peel and slice 2 large bananas, arrange on toasts, slightly overlapping one another. Sprinkle lightly with cinnamon and place under broiler for one or two minutes. Serve 4 triangles to a portion.

551   Blackberry Toast
(Serves 6)

Any kind of canned berries, including cherries may be prepared in this way.

Heat a can of blackberries and sweeten them to taste. Pour into a bowl, and place on top of 12 triangles of bread and butter, crusts removed. Dust the triangles well with powdered sugar, grate a little nutmeg over and serve hot with cream flavored with sherry or lemon, or any kind of desired flavoring.

552   Butterscotch Toast
(Serves 6)

Toast triangles of bread, crusts removed on one side. Spread untoasted side with a mixture of creamed butter and brown sugar and set under broiler until mixture is hot and bubbly. Serve very hot, sprinkled with cinnamon.

553   Cheese and Bacon Toast

As many as required. You may use any kind of toasted bread, from plain bread to fruit bread, but each portion should be composed of two slices of bread of different variety. A good seller for either breakfast or luncheon.

Have ready uniform slices of say white and graham toast. Place a slice of American cheese on each piece of toast. Place a thin slice of bacon on the cheese. Place in broiler until bacon is brown and cheese melted. Serve immediately and bubbling, sprinkled with paprika or cinnamon.

554 **Cheese Toast**
(Serves 6)

Cut ½ lb. American or any other kind of other fat cheese into small pieces. Place in a greased pan. Sprinkle with mixed 1 teaspoon salt, ½ generous teaspoon of prepared mustard and 1 teaspoon of paprika. Now beat 1 whole egg slightly, add ¾ to 1 cup of hot milk (stock may be used) and pour over melted cheese. The liquid used should barely cover the cheese. Bake in a moderate oven (350 deg. F.) 10 to 15 minutes, until cheese is melted and a slightly brown crust has formed. Place a portion size upon any kind of freshly made toast, cut in triangles or quartered.

555 **Cheese Toast Farmer Style**
(Serves 6)

Combine ½ cup of cold milk, ½ teaspoon salt and 3 slightly beaten whole eggs. Put a slice of American or Swiss cheese between 2 slices of bread, crusts removed. Dip into egg mixture and sauté in hot bacon drippings until golden brown on both sides. If desired sharp, spread cheese with prepared mustard before covering with bread.

556 **Cherry Toast I**
(Serves 2)

Heat a small can of pitted cherries or use fresh cherries in season. Cut fresh toast sandwich bread, or any kind of fruit or nut bread into thick fingers—about 2½ inches long, and an inch thick, and toast them quickly in a hot oven, so they are brown on the outside and remain soft inside. Put the hot cherries in a dish, arrange the toast fingers over them and serve with slightly sweetened cream.

557 **Cherry Toast II**
(Serves 2)

Heat ¾ cup canned red pitted cherries with 2 generous tablespoons of sugar mixed with 1 tablespoon of flour, and cook for a few minutes, stirring almost constantly. Flavor with cinnamon to taste. Dip 2 slices of bread, crusts removed, in mixture of beaten egg and milk and brown both sides in butter or bacon drippings. Pour the cherry sauce over the toast.

558 Cinnamon French Toast
As many as required. Two slices to a portion.

To a mixture of beaten egg and milk, add 1 tablespoon of ground cinnamon. Dip two slices of bread, crusts removed, in this mixture, then in flour. Fry in deep fat. Serve with jelly.

559 Cinnamon Toast I
As many as required. Two slices of bread to a portion.

Cut two slices of bread into 1¼-inch thick slices. Remove the crusts; cut each slice into three strips, making oblong blocks. Toast on all sides in oven (not in the broiler or toaster). Dip in melted butter and then roll quickly in a mixture of ½ cup confectioner's sugar and 2 tablespoons cinnamon. Serve very hot. The bread may not be cut into strips if desired.

560 Cinnamon Toast II
As many as required. Two slices of toast to a portion.

Toast two slices of any kind of bread on one side, spread untoasted side with a mixture of 1 tablespoon butter, ¼ cup (scant) powdered sugar, and 1½ to 2 teaspoons of ground cinnamon, creamed well together. Place under flame of broiler and broil until mixture bubbles. Serve sizzling hot.

561 Cinnamon Honey Toast
As many as required. Two slices of toast to a portion.

Mix 2 teaspoons cinnamon with ¼ generous cup of strained honey. Spread on hot buttered toast. Serve very hot.

562 Cinnamon Raisin Toast
Proceed as indicated for No. 560, substituting raisin bread, toasted, for plain bread. Serve sizzling hot.

563   English Toast

As many as required. Two slices of toast to a portion.

Cut plain bread as usual, remove the crusts, lightly toast beneath broiler flame on both sides. Butter the toast quickly and spread with a mixture of 3 tablespoons cream cheese and 1 tablespoon orange marmalade. Serve at once, and as hot as possible.

564   English Muffins

IMPORTANT.—English muffins *should never be cut.* They should be toasted before they are opened. Before toasting, gently break the edges so that after toasting they can be readily and easily pulled apart. Butter on the inside and put in the oven to be kept hot. Like mutton chops their merit consists in their being served as hot as possible. English people have them served one at a time, or "hot and hot to follow."

565   Florida Orange Toast I

As many as required. Two slices of toast to a portion.

Mix ¼ scant cup orange juice, grated rind of one medium-sized orange and ½ cup sugar. Spread on sizzling hot buttered toast. Put into oven or under broiler to brown and serve at once as hot as possible.

566   Florida Orange Toast II

As many as required. Two slices of toast to a portion.

Spread hot toast with creamed butter and cut in narrow strips. Heat together ¼ scant cup of orange juice, and 1 generous teaspoon of chopped orange skin or cut into shreds and 1 teaspoon sugar. Bring to the boiling point and just before serving pour over hot toast. Pile criss-cross on hot plate. Serve at once.

567   French Apple Sauce Toast

As many as required. Two slices of toast to a portion.

Cut 2 slices of bread into 1¼-inch thick slices. Remove the crusts; cut each slice into three strips, making oblong block. Toast on all sides in the oven, not under the flame of broiler or toaster. Dip in melted butter, and then roll quickly in thick, hot apple sauce. Serve at once.

568   French Griddle Toast
As many as required. Two slices of toast to a portion.

Dip two slices of at least a day-old bread in mixture of egg and milk, sweeten with a few grains of sugar to taste. Cook on a hot griddle with a little butter on both sides. Serve with either jelly or marmalade (any kind).

569   French Toast Dessert
(Serves 1)

Soak 2 round slices of bread in egg and milk mixture sweetened with a little sugar and a few grains of cinnamon. Brown in butter on both sides. Have canned peach halves heated in oven. Place a half-peach on each round of fried bread, sprinkle with a little cinnamon or ground nut meats. Serve hot with a little cream on the side.

Chopped dates or figs or prunes, or raisins (seedless) in center of each half-peach may be added. Pears (canned) may be substituted for peaches.

570   French Toast Entrée
(Serves 6)

Beat 2 eggs slightly with 2/3 cup milk, season to taste with salt and white pepper. Dip 6 slices of white bread (or other bread). Dip 6 slices of bread in mixture. Brown the bread on both sides on a hot griddle. Sauté 6 slices of drained canned pineapple slices in butter. Fry or broil 12 slices of bacon. Serve toast topped with pineapple slices topped with guava or any other kind of jelly or marmalade and garnish each with 1 strip of cooked bacon. Garnish with watercress. Serve sizzling hot.

571   French Toast With Raisin Bread
(Serves 1)

Remove crusts from raisin bread, cut each slice in half. Dip in egg and milk mixture, sweetened to taste with honey (dip in each piece of raisin bread separately), and brown lightly on both sides in hot butter. If a rough surface is liked, dip each piece of raisin bread into egg and milk mixture sweetened to taste with honey, then into soft fine bread crumbs before browning. Serve with syrup, honey or jelly.

572   Fried Toast
(Serves 1)

Instead of toasting the bread, using two slices to a portion, sauté or fry the bread in bacon fat until crisp. Try serving eggs on this with bacon, of course.

573   Fruit Toast
(Serves 1)

Use diced oranges, pineapple, or ready cut canned fruit in can. Mix three tablespoons of fruit with sugar to taste, heat to boiling point, add a few drops of lemon juice, and pour over freshly made toast. Serve at once.

574   Ginger Toast

As many as required. Serve six strips to a portion.

Have ready bread cut into 1¼-inch thick slices. Remove the crusts; cut each slice into three strips, making oblong blocks. Toast on all sides in the oven, and while hot, spread with a mixture made of chopped preserved ginger, a few drops of lemon juice and a little water and sugar to taste, cooked to the consistency of marmalade. Serve sizzling hot.

575   Honey Cinnamon Toast
(Serves 1)

Toast 2 slices of bread (any kind). Spread with butter and strained honey, sprinkle with coarsely chopped nut meats and generously with cinnamon. Serve very hot.

576   Jelly Toast Roll
(Serves 6)

Cut crusts of 12 slices from any kind of bread at least one day old. Spread with jelly. Roll up as for jelly roll. Fasten with toothpicks, place on baking sheet, seam side down and cover with a damp cloth until ready to serve. Toast under medium broiler heat, turning until evenly browned. Serve hot.

577   Jocko Toast

Consists of strips of French bread, tasted in oven then rubbed lightly with garlic. Very appropriate for almost any kind of chowder, fish soup and fish stew.

578   Luncheon Toast
(Serves 6)

Dip each slice of bread in mixture of egg, milk and a little sugar to taste, using 12 slices. Carefully transfer to a hot frying pan or a griddle, greased with butter, using a spatula. Brown on both sides. Serve on a hot platter with apple sauce at sides, and sprinkle powdered sugar mixed with cinnamon over the top. Garnish with bits of jelly. Serve very hot.

579   Maple Sugar Toast

Thinly slice 2 slices of one day old bread and remove the crusts Toast and spread lightly with softened butter and soft maple sugar. Return to the oven until the sugar melts. Serve each slice with a spoonful of whipped cream.

580   Marmalade Almond Toast
(Serves 1)

Remove the crusts from two slices of white bread and toast evenly to golden brown. Butter, then spread generously and evenly with marmalade (any kind). Have hot almonds, unsalted and toasted, ready to sprinkle over marmalade. Serve at once.

581   Marmalade Toast
(Serves 1)

Spread two slices of toasted bread (any kind) with soft butter, then with marmalade (any kind). Heat to bubbling under broiler, serve at once.

582   Melba Toast

As many as required. Serve 6 pieces to a portion

Thinly slice 2 or 3 day old bread with very sharp knife not more than 1/8-inch thick after removing the crusts. Place on rack in a very slow oven (200 deg. F.) and allow to dry crisp thoroughly. Toast will be crisp and a light brown when done.

583   Milk Toast I
(Serves 1)

Use two slices of toast for each serving. Put toast into a bowl which has been heated, the toast may be buttered or not, and pour boiling milk, using 1¼ to 1½ cups over the toast. Season with salt and white pepper and paprika.

584   Milk Toast II
(Serves 1)

Use two slices of toast for each serving. Put toast into bowl which has been heated, and pour 1¼ to 1½ cups of thin white sauce over the toast. Season with salt and pepper and a little paprika, or cinnamon to taste (optional).

585   Peanut Butter Toast
(Serves 1)

Cream together equal quantities of butter and peanut butter, and spread on very hot toast. Serve at once, after cutting from corner to corner, the two slices of toast.

586   Pineapple Cinnamon Toast
(Serves 1)

Drain 3 tablespoons of canned crushed pineapple, reserving the juice for other uses if desired. Combine with 1 generous teaspoon of brown sugar and 1 teaspoon of cinnamon. Spread mixture upon toasted white or whole wheat bread, place under broiler until mixture is slightly glazed.

587   Potted Meat Toast With Egg Sauce
An economical entrée which will serve 4.

Spread 4 slices of any kind of toasted bread with canned potted meat; arrange on individual platter and pour over 2 generous tablespoons of egg sauce, or cheese sauce or tomato sauce, or simply white sauce. Garnish with 1 plain boiled potato, and watercress.

588   Rum Tum Ditty
An economical entrée which will serve 4.

Heat 1 can of condensed tomato soup over hot water and stir in ½ lb. grated American cheese until melted. Add ½ scant teaspoon of dry mustard, then pour this over one slightly beaten egg. Serve hot on toast, cut from corner to corner. Garnish with watercress and a slice of dill pickle.

589   Toasted Coconut Strips
(Serves 1)

Toast 2 slices of bread (any kind on one side, cut into strpis, making 3 strips from each slice. Spread untoasted side with a mixture of creamed butter and brown sugar, in equal parts, and brown in a hot oven. Sprinkle over each strip a little shredded coconut. Serve very hot.

590   Tomato French Toast Cheese Sauce
An economical entrée which will serve 4.

Combine and six thoroughly 1 can of condensed tomato soup with 2 slightly beaten eggs. Remove the crusts from 8 slices of any kind of bread. Dip into tomato mixture which has been seasoned to taste with salt and pepper, and cook until lightly browned in a little hot bacon drippings, turning once. Serve at once covered with cheese sauce, garnished with watercress and a large black olive. Dust with paprika.

591   Water Toast
(Serves 1)

Dip 3 slices of very dry toast in boiling salted water. Spread with butter and serve immediately. Garnish with watercress and 1 slice of tomato.

592 SANDWICH PROFITS CHECKING CHART

The truth about profits in sandwich making may be discovered by referring to the following chart, which reveals the fact that there is an average percentage of profit of well over 50, and sometimes as high as 70 or 80. Also that the cheaper range of materials, which are comparatively less expensive, usually yield a greater profit than expensive and scarcer ones. In other words, a Peanut Butter sandwich with a raw cost of 12 cents per pound makes a profit of 80 per cent, selling at 15 cents, while a sliced white meat chicken sandwich, selling at 60 cents, yields a 40 per cent profit.

For interest and variety put your ingredients on different breads, such as Cream Cheese on Orange-Nut Bread or Corned Beef on Pumpernickel, your trade will appreciate it and your employees will take greater interest in developing and discovering menu items.

The chart of 67 standard sandwiches which follows reveals: (1) The portion sizes of various ingredients; (2) the raw cost; (3) the cooked or prepared cost; (4) the cost per portion; (5) the average cost of bread, butter; (6) other ingredients; (7) the total cost; (8) sale price; (9) profit; (10) percentage of profit; (11) suggested relishes.

By following this chart closely, you can decide which are the profitable numbers to feature.

It is understood that the figures may not be 100 per cent perfect, due to various uncontrollable reasons, such as the seasons of the year, fluctuations of price, proximity to markets, different portion sizes, and others. For instance, the nearer the source of supply, the lower the cost of materials. Sea foods on the coast are considerably cheaper than at the inland markets.

The costs of materials were compiled from figures obtained from the Eastern United States and Middle West. However, the cost may be altered to suit the locality and the particular operator who has a different formulae, or uses additional ingredients. This merely acts as a guide and it is meant to be flexible so that adjustments may be made.

The mathematics involved in this chart are simple enough so that the layman may use them, to calculate his own costs. For example, add the total cost of ingredients like this (using a ham and cheese sandwich as a basis). One ounce of cheese at 24 cents per pound costs .0150 or 1½ cents. One ounce of ham at 50 cents per pound (prepared cost) costs .0312 or 3 cents and 12 hundredths. The total of these, plus bread and butter at .0213 adds up to 6¾ cents.

```
Cheese ................................. .0150
Ham ..................................... .0312
Bread ................................... .0213

Total cost ........................... .0675 or 6¾ cents
```

If the selling price is 20 cents, then by subtraction you get:

```
            .0675
           ───────
            .1325 profit
```

To obtain the percentage of profit, divide .1325 by the sale price and you get an answer of 66 per cent profit.

```
  .20  |      .1325     |  66% profit
        ─     120        ─
               ───
               125
               120
               ───
```

For convenience sake, the listing has been done by dividing sandwiches into eight groups!

                                          Sandwiches numbered
1. Meats .... 1 to 20 inclusive
2. Eggs .... 21 to 23 inclusive
3. Fish and Sea Food .... 24 to 34 inclusive
4. Cheese .... 34 to 41 inclusive
5. Butter and Spread .... 42 to 46 inclusive
6. Fruits .... 47 to 49 inclusive
7. Poultry .... 50 to 54 inclusive
8. Combination (two and three decker
    sandwiches) .... 55 to 67 inclusive

COST TABLE — BREADS — RELISHES

All listed sandwich costs are calculated either with white, whole wheat or rye breads. Special breads usually cost a little more in price, but they are usually of smaller size and consequently require smaller quantities of materials and ingredients.

	Price per Pound	Slices per Pound	Cost per Slice	Cost per Sandwich
White	.08	12	.0066	.0133
Rye	.08	14	.0057	.0114
Whole Wheat	.08	12	.0066	.0133
Raisin Whole Wheat	.08	12	.0066	.0133
Date Nut	.24	20	.0120	.0240
Nut	.24	20	.0120	.0240
Peanut Butter	.15	20	.0075	.0150
Prune	.12	20	.0066	.0120
Cheese	.12	16	.0075	.0150
Rolls	.12 dozen			.0100
English Muffin	.18 dozen			.0150

The use of butter is average, but to figure on the maximum side, take 1/40 of a pound, or one average patty per sandwich. Thus, at 32 cents per pound, the cost per sandwich is .0008 cents.

Garnishes are not included in this combination. They vary widely in quality, quantity, and cost, but may easily be added, to determine the actual cost of the sandwich as served. Here are a few of those used generally:

	Cost		Cost Each	Portion	Cost per Sandwich
1 Dill Pickles	$0.45 per gallon	(100 size)	.0010	¼	.0010
2 Sweet Pickles	2.00 per gallon	(200 size)	.0100	1	.0100
3 Pickle Rings	2.00 per gallon	400 pieces	.0050	2	.0100
4 Gherkins	1.60 per gallon	320 pieces	.0050	2	.0100
5 Burr Gherkins	2.50 per gallon	300 pieces	.0083	2	.0166
6 Olives	1.50 per gallon	300 pieces	.0050	2	.0100
7 Cole Slaw	.25 per gallon			2 ounces	.0039
8 Chow Chow	1.50 per gallon			1 ounce	.0117
9 Relish	1.00 per gallon			1 ounce	.0078
10 Potato Salad	.10 per pound			2 ounces	.0080
11 French Fried Potatoes	.10 per pound			2 ounces	.0080
12 Radishes	.05 per bunch		.0025	6 ounces	.0050

In the chart, the following symbols are used: M—symbolizes mayonnaise at $1.00 per gallon; L—symbolizes lettuce at an average of 10 cents per head; and 10 sandwiches per head; GP—symbolizes green peppers (chopped); Pim—symbolizes pimientos; TS—symbolizes tartare sauce.

—By BAYARD D. EVANS.

SANDWICH COST TABLE FOR PROFESSIONALS

		Portion Ounces	Raw Cost Per Pound	Prepared Cost Per Pound	Cost Per Portion	Bread and Butter	Other Ingredients	Total Cost	Selling Price	Profit	% Profit	Suggested Relishes
Meat 1	Ham, Boiled	1 oz.	.40	.50	.0312	.0213	L.0050	.0575	.10	.0425	42	Pickle Rings
2		1½ oz.	.40	.50	.0468	.0213	L.0050	.0731	.15	.0769	5-	Sweet Pickles
3	Ham, Minced	1 oz.	.30	.30	.0187	.0213	L.0050	.0450	.10	.0550	55	Gherkins
4	Ham, Fried	1 oz.	.24	.40	.0250	.0213	L.0050	.0513	.15	.0987	66	Dill Pickles
5		1½ oz.	.24	.40	.0375	.0213	L.0050	.0638	.20	.1362	68	Dill Pickles
6	Deviled Smithfield	1 oz.	1.25	1.25	.0781	.0213	L.0050	.1044	.25	.1456	58	Chow Chow
7	Lamb Shoulder	1½ oz.	.18	.40	.0375	.0213		.0588	.20	.1412	71	Burr Gherkins
8	Veal Cutlet	1½ oz.	.19	.45	.0421	.0213		.0634	.25	.1866	75	Relish
9	Pork Loin	2½ oz.	.21	.42	.0655	.0213	L.0050	.0918	.25	.1582	63	Cole Slaw
10	Corned Beef	2 oz.	.20	.36	.0450	.0213	L.0050	.0713	.25	.1787	71	Cole Slaw
11	Tongue	1½ oz.	.26	.45	.0421	.0213	L.0050	.0684	.20	.1316	66	Pot. Sal. Rel.
12	Liverwurst	1½ oz.	.22	.22	.0205	.0213		.0418	.15	.1082	72	Dill Pickle
13	Salami (soft)	1½ oz.	.32	.32	.0300	.0213		.0513	.15	.0987	66	Relish
14	Bologna	1½ oz.	.18		.0168	.0213		.0381	.15	.1119	75	Dill Pickle
15	Frankfurter	2 oz	.22	.22	.0274	.0180		.0454	.10	.0546	55	Cole Slaw
16	Bacon	1½ oz.	.32	.32	.0300	.0213	L.0050	.0563	.20	.1437	72	Relish
17	Hamburg	2 oz	.20	.20	.0250	.0180		.0430	.15	.1070	71	Potato Salad
18	Cubed Steak	2 oz	.30	.30	.0374	.0213		.0587	.20	.1413	71	French Fries
19	Ham and	1 oz.	.40	.50	.0312							Relish
	Tongue	1 oz.	.26	.45	.0281	.0213	L.0050	.0856	.25	.1644	66	Radishes
20	Pork and	1 oz	.21	.42	.0262							Cole Slaw
	Ham	1 oz.	.40	.50	.0312	.0213	L.0050	.0837	.25	.1663	67	Radishes
Egg 21	Fried or Boiled	1 egg	.24 dz		.0200	.0213	L.0050	.0463	.15	.1037	69	Relish
22	Chopped and Mayonnaise	1 egg	.24 dz		0200	.0213	M.0050 L.0050	.0513	15	.0987	66	

SANDWICH COST TABLE FOR PROFESSIONALS

		Portion Ounces	Raw Cost Per Pound	Prepared Cost Per Pound	Cost Per Portion	Bread and Butter	Other Ingredients	Total Cost	Selling Price	Profit	% Profit	Suggested Relishes
23	Egg Salad Green Pepper Pimientos	1 egg	.24 dz	—	.0200		M.0050 GP.0050 Pim.0030	.0543	15	.0957	64	Gherkins
Fish 24	Sardine	1¾ oz	.64	.64	.0700	.0213	L.0050	.0963	.20	.1037	52	Dill Pickle
25	Salmon	2 oz	.24	.24	.0300	.0213	L.0050	.0563	.15	.0937	62	Dill Pickle
26	Tuna	1½ oz	.48	.48	.0450	.0213	L.0050	.0713	.25	.1787	71	Gherkin Olive
27	Crab Meat	1½ oz	.48	.48	.0450	.0213	L.0050 M.0050	.0763	.25	.1737	69	Relish
28	Oyster	3 oysters	.02 each	.02	.0600	.0213		.0913	.25	.1587	63	Cole Slaw
29	Fillet of Sole	2 oz	.25	—	.0312	.0213	TS.0050 L.0050	.0625	20	.1375	69	Cole Slaw Potato Salad
30	Crab Salad	1 oz	.48	.48	.0300	.0213	M.0050 L.0050	.0813	25	.1687	67	Burr
	Egg Salad	1 egg	.24 dz	.24 dz	.0200	—				—	—	Gherkins
31	Shrimp Salad	2 oz	.20	.32	.0400	.0213	M.0050 L.0050	.0913	.25	.1587	63	Sweet
	Egg Salad	1 egg	.24 dz	.24 dz	.0200	—		—	—	—	—	Pickles
32	Salmon Salad	1½ oz	.25	.25	.0234	.0213	M.0050 L.0050	.0747	.20	.1253	63	Dill
	Egg Salad	1 egg	.24 dz	.24 dz	.0200	—		—	—	—	—	Pickles
33	Tuna Salad	1 oz	.48	—	.0300	.0213	M.0050 L.0050	.0813	.25	.1687	67	Olives
	Egg Salad	1 egg	.24 dz	.24 dz	.0200	—		—	—	—	—	Radishes
Cheese 34	American	1 oz.	.24	.24	.0150	.0213	L.0050	.0413	10	.0587	59	Pickle Rings
35	American	1½ oz.	.24	.24	.0225	.0213	L.0050	.0488	15	.1012	67	Pickle Rings
36	Swiss, Imported	1 oz.	.65	.65	.0406	.0213		.0619	.25	.1881	75	Dill Pickles
37	Swiss, Domestic	1 oz	.28	.28	.0175	.0213		.0388	.20	.1612	81	Dill Pickles

SANDWICH COST TABLE FOR PROFESSIONALS

		Portion Ounces	Raw Cost Per Pound	Prepared Cost Per Pound	Cost Per Portion	Bread and Butter	Other Ingredients	Total Cost	Selling Price	Profit	% Profit	Suggested Relishes
38	Cream Cheese and Pineapple	1 oz. ½ oz.	.24 .32	.24 .32	.0150 .0100	.0213 —	— —	.0463 —	.25 —	.2037 —	81 —	Burr Gherkins —
39	Cream Cheese and Jelly	1 oz. ½ oz.	.24 .16	.24 —	.0150 .0050	.0213 —	— —	.0413 —	.25 —	.2087 —	83 —	Sweet Pickles —
40	Cream Cheese and Bacon	1 oz. 2 slices 1 oz.	.24 .32	.24 .32	.0150 .0200	.0213 —	— —	.0563 —	.25 —	.1937 —	77 —	Sweet Pickle —
41	Cream Cheese and Canadian Bacon	1 oz. 1 oz.	.24 .48	.24 .48	.0150 .0300	.0213 —	— —	.0663 —	.30 —	.2337 —	78 —	Burr Gherkins —
Butters												
42	Peanut Butter	1½ oz.	.12	.12	.0113	.0213	—	.0326	.15	.1174	78	Gherkins
43	Peanut Butter and Banana	1 oz. ½ B.	.12 .02 ea	.12 .02 ea	.0075 .0100	.0213 —	L.0050 —	.0438 —	.20 —	.1607 —	80 —	Gherkins —
44	Olive Butter	1¼ oz.	.34	.34	.0265	.0213	L.0050	.0528	.20	.1472	74	Dill Pickle
45	Olive and Nut	1¼ oz.	.32	.32	.0250	.0213	L.0050	.0513	.20	.1487	74	Dills
46	Apple Butter	2 oz.	.10	.10	.0124	.0213	L.0050	.0387	.15	.1113	74	Gherkins
Fruit												
47	Banana and Pecans	½ B. ¼ oz.	.02 ea .32	.02 ea .32	.0100 .0050	.0213 —	M.0050 L.0050	.0463 —	.20 —	.1537 —	77 —	Burr Gherkins —
48	Fig and Pecan	3 Figs ¼ oz.	.15 .32	.15 .32	.0279 .0050	.0213 —	M.0050 L.0050	.0642 —	.20 —	.1358 —	68 —	Pickle Rings —
49	Date and Apple	3 oz. ½	.14 .03 ea	.14 .03 ea	.0261 .0150	.0213 —	M.0050 L.0050	.0724 —	.20 —	.1276 —	64 —	Olives —

INDEX

	Page
Almond Butter	98
Almond Marmalade on Toast	36
Almond-Marshmallow-Fig Date Filling on Toast or Bread	36
Almond-Peanut Butter on Bread	35
Almond-Pineapple on Toast	35
American Cheese AND Broiled Ham Sandwich	18
American Cheese Butter	98
American Cheese AND Caviar Sandwich	17
American Cheese Dream Sandwich	18
American Cheese-Dried Beef AND Tomatoes	18
American Cheese AND Fried Bacon Sandwich	18
American Cheese AND Nut Filling	104
American Cheese AND Green Pepper Sandwich	19
American Cheese-Ham AND Tomato on Toast	36
American Cheese AND Peanut Butter Sandwich	19
American Cheese-Peanut Butter AND Jelly on Bread	36
American Cheese Sandwich	18
American Cheese AND Spinach Sandwich	19
American Cheese AND Tomato Sandwich	19
Anchovy Butter	98
Anchovy and Parmesan Cheese Filling	104
Apple Sauce Butter	98
Apple-Nut-Fig AND Shredded Pineapple on Rye	36
Apple-Peanut Butter Filling AND Pineapple Slice on Toast	36
Apple and Peanut Butter Filling	104
Apricot Butter	98
Apricot Filling I	105
Apricot Filling II	105
Apricot-Ham on Toast	35
Asparagus Tips-Tomato AND Cole Slaw on Whole Wheat	36
Avocado Filling	105
Bacon AND Banana on Toast	37
Bacon-Bean Salad AND Tomato on White	37
Bacon-Chicken AND Anchovies on Toast	37
Bacon-Chicken-Green Pepper AND Tomato on Toast	37

	Page
Bacon-Chicken Livers AND Tomato on Toast	37
Bacon-Cress AND Salami on White	39
Bacon-Cucumber AND Asparagus Tips on Rye	39
Bacon-Green Pepper AND Tomato on Toast	37
Bacon-Orange Marmalade AND Banana on Rye	37
Bacon-Onion AND Tomato on Rye	37
Bacon-Potato Salad AND Tomato on Rye	38
Bacon-Potato Salad AND Egg Salad on White	38
Bacon-Potato Salad AND Ham on Toast	38
Bacon-Swiss Cheese AND Egg-Anchovy on Toast	38
Bacon-Swiss Cheese AND Tongue-Tomato on White	38
Bacon-Swiss Cheese AND Turkey on Toasted Rye	38
Bacon-Tomato-Cole Slaw AND Swiss Cheese on Toast	39
Bacon-Tomato AND Onion-Caviar on Toast	38
Bacon-Tomato AND Liverwurst on White	39
Bacon AND Tomato Sandwich.	7
Bacon-Tomato AND Sardine on Rye	39
Bacon-Tomato AND Vegetable Salad on Whole Wheat	39
Bacon-Watercress AND Beef Salad on Rye	40
Baked Beans Cheesewitch	7
Baked Beans Horseradish Filling	105
Baked Beans Rarebit Sandwich	7
Baltimore Toast	116
Banana Cinnamon Toast	117
Beef Salad-Cole Slaw AND Tomato on White	40
Beef Salad-Pickle Relish AND American Cheese on White.	40
Blackberry Toast	117
Boiled Beef Sandwich	7
Broiled Ham Sandwich	8
Broiled Tomato Sandwich	8
Butterscotch Toast	117
Camembert Sandwich	20
Canadian Cheese AND Apple Sandwich	20
Cape Cod Sandwich	8
Carrot Filling	106

INDEX—(Continued)

	Page
Catsup Butter	98
Caviar Butter	98
Caviar-Onion AND Tomato on Toast	40
Cheese and Bacon Toast	117
CHEESE SANDWICHES AND CHEESE COMBINATION FILLINGS	15
Cheese	15
Cheese Toast	118
Cheese Toast Farmer Style	118
Cherry Toast I	118
Cherry Toast II	118
Chicken-Asparagus Tips AND Bacon-Tomato on Toast	41
Chicken-Bacon AND Green Pepper-Tomato on Toast	40
Chicken-Bacon AND Tomato-Nut Meats on Rye	41
Chicken - Bacon AND Tomato - Olives on White	40
Chicken-Bacon AND Tongue-Tomato on Whole Wheat	41
Chicken Briarcliff Manor Sandwich	8
Chicken-Celery-Lettuce AND Bacon Tomato on Rye	40
Chicken Filling	106
Chicken Filling II	106
Chicken-Green Pepper AND Tomato-Anchovy on Rye	41
Chicken-Lettuce AND Jelly-Cress on Raisin Bread	41
Chicken-Lettuce AND Egg-Lettuce on White	44
Chicken-Lettuce AND Pineapple-Red Cabbage on Toast	44
Chicken Livers-Bacon AND Tomato on Nut Bread	44
Chicken Livers - Fried Tomato AND Bacon-Cucumber on Toast	44
Chicken Livers-Red Cole Slaw AND Tomato on Raisin Bread	44
Chicken-Nut Meats AND Jelly-Lettuce on Pumpernickel	41
Chicken Salad-Bacon AND Tomato Relish on Nut Bread	42
Chicken Salad-Beets AND Tongue-Tomato on White	43
Chicken Salad-Cole Slaw AND Ham-Tomato on Toasted Rye	43
Chicken Salad - Cucumber AND Cream Cheese - Anchovy on Pumpernickel	44
Chicken Salad-Green Pepper AND Swiss Cheese - Tomato on Toasted Rye	42
Chicken Salad AND Ham-Swiss Cheese on Pumpernickel	42
Chicken Salad-Olives AND American Cheese-Tomato on Toast	43
Chicken Salad - Pimientos AND Roast Beef-Pickle on Toast	43
Chicken Salad-Tomato AND Anchovy-Lettuce on Rye	42
Chicken Salad-Tomato AND Asparagus Tips on White	42
Chicken Salad AND Tomato-Tongue on Boston Brown Bread	42
Chicken Salad-Tomato AND Vegetable Salad on Toast	43
Chicken Sandwich	8
Chili Butter	98
Chive Butter	98
Chutney Butter	98
Cinnamon French Toast	119
Cinnamon Toast I	119
Cinnamon Toast II	119
Cinnamon Honey Toast	119
Cinnamon Raisin Toast	119
CLUB OR THREE-DECKER COMBINATION SANDWICHES	34
COLOR EFFECTS ON SANDWICHES	96
Corned Beef-Apple AND American Cheese - Lettuce on Toasted Raisin Bread	45
Corned Beef-Cabbage Relish AND Pineapple-Lettuce on Toast	46
Corned Beef-Cole Slaw AND Tomato-Lettuce on White	45
Corned Beef - Chopped Spinach AND Cream Cheese on Whole Wheat	46
Corned Beef-Dill AND Pickled Beets-Lettuce on Rye	45
Corned Beef Hash Sandwich	9
Corned Beef - Horseradish AND Tomato-Cress on White	45
Corned Beef-Onion Slices AND Swiss Cheese-Cress on Toasted Rye	45
Corned Beef Sandwich	8
Cost Tables	128
Cottage Cheese AND Carrot Sandwich	20
Cottage Cheese AND Cherry Preserves Sandwich	20
Cottage Cheese AND Cinnamon Sandwich	20
Cottage Cheese Filling	106
Cottage Cheese-Honey AND Nut Sandwich	21
Cottage Cheese AND Marmalade Sandwich	21

INDEX—(Continued)

Cottage Cheese AND Olive Sandwiches 21
Cottage Cheese AND Raisins Sandwich 21
Crab Meat - Apple Mayonnaise AND Sliced Pineapple on Toasted Raisin Bread 48
Crab Meat-Curried Mayonnaise AND Sardine-Lettuce on Toasted Rye 48
Crab Meat Filling 105
Crab Meat-Ham Mayonnaise AND Banana-Lettuce on White .. 48
Crab Meat Mayonnaise AND Baked Beans Salad on Whole Wheat 48
Crab Meat Mayonnaise AND Cucumber-Cress on Toast .. 48
Crab Meat Mayonnaise-Cucumber AND Tomato-Lettuce on Toasted Rye 46
Crab Meat Mayonnaise AND Salmon-Lettuce on White .. 48
Crab Meat Mayonnaise-Tomato AND Egg Salad - Cress on Toast 46
Crab Meat Mayonnaise-Tomato AND Dill-Lettuce on Raisin Bread 47
Crab Meat Mayonnaise AND String Beans Salad - Lettuce on Toast 47
Crab Meat Nut Mayonnaise AND Tongue-Lettuce on Toast ... 47
Crab Meat-Olives AND Tomato-Lettuce on Nut Bread 46
Crab Meat-Raw Spinach AND Egg Salad-Lettuce on White 47
Crab Meat-Shrimp Mayonnaise AND Vegetable Salad on Toasted Rye 47
Creamed Cheese 22
Cream Cheese AND Almond Sandwiches 22
Cream Cheese AND Apple Sandwich 22
Cream Cheese AND Apricot Sandwich 22
Cream Cheese AND Asparagus Tips Sandwich 23
Cream Cheese AND Banana Filling 107
Cream Cheese AND Beet Sandwich 23
Cream Cheese AND Caraway Seeds Sandwich 23
Cream Cheese AND Celery Sandwich 24
Cream Cheese - Celery AND Cherry Sandwiches 24

Cream Cheese-Celery AND Dates Sandwich 24
Cream Cheese-Chives AND Pineapple Filling 107
Cream Cheese-Cottage Cheese AND Nuts Sandwich 24
Cream Cheese AND Cucumber Sandwiches 24
Cream Cheese AND Fig Sandwich 25
Cream Cheese Filling 106
Cream Cheese AND Grape Nuts Sandwich 25
Cream Cheese AND Honey Filling . 107
Cream Cheese AND Honey Sandwich 25
Cream Cheese AND Horseradish Sandwich 25
Cream Cheese AND Jelly Sandwich 25
Cream Cheese-Horseradish AND Nuts Sandwich 26
Cream Cheese AND Marmalade Sandwich 26
Cream Cheese AND Olive Sandwich 26
Cream Cheese - Pimiento AND Walnuts Sandwich 26
Cream Cheese AND Pineapple Sandwich 26
Cream Cheese-Raisin AND Green Pepper Sandwiches 27
Cream Cheese AND Sardine Sandwich 27
Cream Cheese AND Watercress Sandwich 27
Creamed Hamburger Filling .. 107
Creamed Tuna Sandwich 9
Cress Butter 99
Cube Steak Sandwich 9

Date-Cherry-Pineapple-Nut Mayonnaise AND Toasted Marshmallow-Shredded Coconut on Toasted Rye 49
Date - Nut Meats Mayonnaise AND Ham-Lettuce on Toast. 49
Date-Peanut-Apple Mayonnaise AND Pineapple-Cress on White 49
Denver Sandwich 9
Deviled Cheese Sandwiches ... 28
Deviled Egg-Sardine Salad AND Bacon-Tomato on Pumpernickel 50
Deviled Egg-Chicken Salad AND Spanish Onion-Cress on Toast 50
Deviled Egg-Crab Meat Salad AND Green Onion (or Scallions)-Lettuce on Toast ... 50

INDEX—(Continued)

Deviled Egg-Sardine Salad AND Tomato - Lettuce on Boston Brown Bread 49
Deviled Egg-Salmon Salad AND Green Pepper-Lettuce on Toast 50
Deviled Egg-Shrimp Salad AND Tongue-Cress on Toast 50
DO'S AND DON'TS IN MAKING SANDWICHES 4
Dried Beef AND American Cheese Filling 107
Dried Beef Filling Country Style . 108
Dried Beef AND Horseradish Filling 108
Dried Beef AND Peanut Butter Filling 108

Edam Cheese Sandwich 28
Egg Mayonnaise Filling 108
Egg Salad-Anchovy AND Knockwurst-Cole Slaw-Lettuce on Rye or Pumpernickel 56
Egg Salad-Anchovy AND Tomato-Cress on Toast 54
Egg Salad-Anchovy AND Vegetable Salad on Rye 55
Egg Salad-Asparagus Tips AND Ham-Cheese-Lettuce on Whole Wheat 51
Egg Salad-Bacon AND Tomato-Anchovy-Lettuce on Toasted Whole Wheat 54
Egg Salad-Bacon AND Tomato-Green Pepper-Lettuce on Toast 53
Egg Salad - Bacon AND Swiss Cheese-Cress on White 53
Egg Salad-Bacon AND Tomato-Anchovy Filets - Lettuce on Boston Brown Bread 53
Egg Salad-Bologna AND Tomato-Lettuce on Rye 53
Egg Salad-Chopped Olives AND T o m a t o - Anchovy-Lettuce on Toast 51
Egg Salad - Cole Slaw AND Chicken-Lettuce on White 54
Egg Salad-Cress AND Tomato-Cream Cheese-Walnut on White 55
Egg Salad-Olives AND Swiss Cheese - Anchovy - Lettuce on Toast 55
Egg Salad-Red Cole Slaw AND Tongue - Tomato - Lettuce on Raisin Bread 54
Egg Salad-Green Pepper Rings AND Frankfurter-Lettuce on Rye 55

Egg Salad-Green Pepper AND Tomato - Anchovy - Lettuce on Whole Wheat 51
Egg Salad-Green Pepper Rings AND Tuna Fish-Lettuce on Rye 54
Egg Salad-Green Pepper Rings AND Sardines-Nut Meats on Whole Wheat 52
Egg Salad-Ham AND Tomato-Lettuce (or cress) on Toasted Roll 51
Egg Salad - Minced Ham AND Liverwurst-Tomato-Lettuce on Pumpernickel 53
Egg Salad-Pimientos AND Chicken-Bacon-Lettuce on Toast. 52
Egg Salad-Roast Beef AND Tomato-Anchovy-Lettuce on White 51
Egg Salad-Roast Pork AND Tomato-Lettuce on White 52
Egg Salad-Sardines-Cress AND Tomato-Lettuce on Toast .. 52
Egg Salad-Tomato AND Asparagus Tips-Lettuce on White . 55
Egg Salad-Tomato AND Pineapple-Lettuce on Toasted Raisin Bread 54
Egg Salad-Tomato AND Salmon-Olive Meats-Lettuce on Rye . 52
Egg Salad-Tomato AND Sliced Spanish Onion-Caviar on Toast 56
Egg Salad-Tomato AND String Beans Salad-Lettuce on Rye 55
Egg Salad-Tongue AND American Cheese-Lettuce on Rye . 51
Egg Salad-Watercress AND Anchovy-Bacon-Lettuce on White 50
Egg Salad-Watercress AND Pickle Relish-Asparagus Tips on Rye 56
Egg (sliced)-Anchovy AND Tomato-Lettuce on Pumpernickel 59
Egg (sliced)-A n c h o v y AND Tongue-Watercress on Rye . 59
Egg (sliced)-Bacon-Lettuce AND Baked Beans-Lettuce on Toast 58
Egg (sliced)-Bacon AND Lobster Salad-Lettuce on Toast or Rye 60
Egg (sliced)-Bacon-Olive AND Potato Nut Salad-Lettuce on White 59
Egg (sliced)-Bacon-Lettuce AND Tomato-Cress on Toast 58
Egg (sliced) - Chopped Celery-Olives AND Sardine-Lettuce on White 56

INDEX—(Continued)

Egg (sliced)-Chicken Liver AND American Cheese-Cress on Toast 59
Egg (sliced)-Cole Slaw AND Tomato-Green Pepper Rings on Toasted Rye 57
Egg (sliced)-Cucumber AND Banana-Cheese-Lettuce on Date Bread 60
Egg (sliced)-Ham AND String Beans Salad-Lettuce on Toast 57
Egg (sliced)-Minced Ham AND Nut Slaw-Cress on Toast 60
Egg (sliced)-Pimiento Rings AND Sliced Ham-Relish-Lettuce on Rye 58
Egg (sliced)-Red Cole Slaw AND Potato Salad-Lettuce on Rye 57
Egg (sliced) - Shredded Lettuce (dressed) AND Tomato-Cress on Raisin Bread 56
Egg (sliced)-Shrimp Salad AND Chicken-Lettuce on White 59
Egg (sliced)-Swiss Cheese AND Ham-Tomato-Lettuce on Toasted Rye 57
Egg (sliced)-Tomato-Cole Slaw AND Ham Salad-Lettuce on Rye 57
Egg (sliced)-Tomato-Cress AND Chicken Salad-Lettuce on White 57
Egg (sliced)-Tomato-Green Pepper Rings AND Salmon Salad on Toasted Rye 58
Egg (sliced) - Tomato - Lettuce AND Tuna Fish Salad-Lettuce on Boston Brown Bread 58
Egg Yolk Butter 99
English Muffins 120
English Toast 120

Far East Filling 108
Fig AND Date Filling 109
Fish Cake Sandwich 9
Fish Roe Mayonnaise Filling 109
Florida Orange Toast I 120
Florida Orange Toast II 120
Fluffy Peanut Butter Filling 109
French Apple Sauce Toast 120
French Cream Cheese Sandwich 28
French Griddle Toast 121
French Toast Dessert 121
French Toast Entree 121
French Toast with Raisin Bread 121
Fried Chicken Sandwich 10
Fried Egg Sandwich 10
Fried Egg and Green Pepper Sandwich 10
Fried Egg AND Onion Sandwich 10
Fried Egg AND Tomato Sandwich 10
Fried Ham Sandwich 10
Fried Toast 122
Fruit Toast 122

Garlic Butter 99
Ginger and Date Filling 109
Ginger Toast 122
Green Pepper Butter 99

Ham-American Cheese AND Tomato-Anchovy-Lettuce on Toasted Rye 62
Ham-American Cheese AND Tomato-Cress on Toasted Whole Wheat 62
Ham-Cole Slaw AND Tomato-Lettuce on White 60
Ham-Cream Cheese AND Turkey-Cranberry-Lettuce on Toasted Whole Wheat 64
Ham-Cress AND Bacon-Tomato-Lettuce on Rye 63
Ham-Cress AND Potato Salad-Lettuce on Pumpernickel 62
Ham-Currant Jelly AND Tomato-Lettuce on Orange Date Bread 61
Ham-Dill Pickle AND Tomato-Lettuce on Rye 62
Ham AND Egg Sandwich 11
Ham (minced)-Egg Salad AND Tomato-Lettuce on White 65
Ham-Giblets AND Egg Filling 110
Ham - Horseradish AND Green Pepper Rings-Lettuce on Boston Brown Bread 61
Ham - Horseradish AND Potato Salad-Cress on Rye 62
Ham AND Jelly Filling 110
Ham - Liederkranz Cheese AND Tomato-Lettuce on Rye 63
Ham AND Mayonnaise Filling 110
Ham-Mustard Pickle AND Potato Nut Salad-Lettuce on Rye 63
Ham AND Raw Vegetable Filling 110
Ham-Pickle Relish AND Asparagus Tips-Lettuce on Rye 61
Ham-Potato Salad AND Tomato-Cress on Rye 61
Ham-Potato Salad AND Tomato-Pickle-Lettuce on White 64
Ham Salad-Anchovy AND Tomato-Shredded Lettuce on Rye 69

INDEX—(Continued)

	Page
Ham Salad - Artichoke Bottom AND Tomato-Anchovy-Lettuce on White or Rye	67
Ham Salad-Asparagus Tips AND Tomato-Cress on Toast	66
Ham Salad-Corn Salad AND Chicken-Tomato-Lettuce on Toast	68
Ham Salad-Cress AND Tomato-Anchovy-Lettuce on Rye	66
Ham Salad-Dill AND Tomato-Cucumber-Lettuce on Rye	67
Ham Salad-Gherkin AND Vegetable Salad-Lettuce on Rye	68
Ham Salad-Green Pepper Rings AND Potato Salad-Lettuce on Rye	66
Ham Salad-Pimiento AND Navy Beans Salad-Lettuce on White	68
Ham Salad-Lettuce AND Tomato-Lettuce on Toast	68
Ham Salad-Lettuce AND Tomato-Cress on Toast	65
Ham Salad-Pickle Relish AND American Cheese-Tomato on Pumpernickel	65
Ham Salad-Pickle Relish AND Bacon-Tomato-Lettuce on Rye	65
Ham Salad-Pickle Relish AND Tomato-Swiss Cheese on Rye	65
Ham Salad-Raw Spinach AND Bermuda Onion-Egg Salad on White	67
Ham Salad-Red Cole Slaw AND Tomato-Horseradish-Cress on Rye	66
Ham Salad-Shredded Pineapple AND Tomato-Lettuce on Rye	68
Ham Salad - Sliced Egg AND Caviar-Lettuce on Toasted Rye	67
Ham-Salad-Swiss Cheese AND Apple-Lettuce on White or Rye	66
Ham Salad-Tomato AND Potato Salad-Lettuce on Whole Wheat	66
Ham Salad-Tomato AND Spanish Onion-Caviar Lettuce on Whole Wheat	67
Ham-Swiss Cheese AND Bacon-Tomato-Lettuce on Toast	63
Ham-Tomato AND Bermuda Onion-Celery Salad-Lettuce on Toasted Rye	64
Ham-Tomato-Cucumber AND Egg Salad - Liverwurst - Lettuce on Toast	64
Ham-Tomato AND String Beans Salad-Lettuce on Whole Wheat	63
Ham-Tomato-Celery Green AND Pepper Relish-Lettuce on Toast	64
Ham-Tomato AND Tongue-Swiss Cheese-Lettuce on Rye	61
Ham AND Walnut Meats Filling	110
Ham AND Swiss Cheese Sandwich	11
Ham-Swiss Cheese AND Tomato-Lettuce on White	60
Hamburger-American Cheese AND Bacon-Lettuce on Whole Wheat	72
Hamburger-Bean Salad AND Orange Marmalade-Nut Cress on Orange Date Bread	71
Hamburger-Bermuda Onion AND Ham-Dill-Lettuce on Rye	69
Hamburger-Broiled Ham AND Potato Salad-Nut-Lettuce on Rye	71
Hamburger-Chopped Bacon AND Swiss Cheese-Lettuce on Toast	69
Hamburger - Cress AND Cream Cheese-Raspberry Jam-Lettuce on Raisin Bread	71
Hamburger-Cress AND Egg Salad-Lettuce on Toast	69
Hamburger-Dill AND Bermuda Onion-Tomato-Lettuce on Rye	72
Hamburger-Fried Tomato AND String Beans Salad-Lettuce on Toast	71
Hamburger-HorseradishAND American Cheese-Lettuce on Toast	72
Hamburger-Lettuce AND Chicken Salad-Lettuce on White	70
Hamburger - Liederkranz Cheese AND Tongue-Tomato-Lettuce on Pumpernickel or Rye	70
Hamburger-Mustard Pickles AND Pineapple-Lettuce on Rye	69
Hamburger-Pickle Relish AND Cucumber Salad-Lettuce on Rye	72
Hamburger Sandwich	11
Hamburger-Sauerkraut AND Tomato-Bacon-Lettuce on Pumpernickel or Rye	70
Hamburger-Smothered Onions AND American Cheese-Lettuce on Boston Brown Bread	71
Hamburger - Shredded Pineapple AND Tomato-Lettuce on Raisin Bread	69
Hamburger-Sliced Egg AND Orange Marmalade-Lettuce on Nut Bread	70
Hamburger-Tomato AND Curried Egg-Lettuce on Toast	70
Herring Butter	99
Herring Filets - Bermuda Onion AND Tomato-Cress on Rye	74

INDEX—(Continued)

Herring Filets-Cucumber Salad AND American Cheese - Cress on Whole Wheat Bread .. 73
Herring Filets-Dill AND Tuna Fish Salad-Lettuce on Rye . 74
Herring Filets-Potato Salad AND Tomato - Lettuce on Toasted Pumpernickel 74
Herring Filets-Red Cole Slaw AND Bermuda Onion-Pimiento on Rye 73
Herring Filets-String Beans Salad AND Tomato - Cress on Toasted Rye 74
Herring Filets-Tomato AND Crab Meat Salad on Pumpernickel 73
Herring Filets-Tomato AND Green Pepper Rings-Dill-Cress on Rye 73
Herring Filets-Tomato AND Salmon Salad-Lettuce on Toasted Rye 74
Herring Salad-Lettuce AND Swiss Cheese-Lettuce on Rye 73
Honey-Almond Paste AND Cream Cheese-Lettuce on Orange Bread 75
Honey-Banana AND Cream Cheese-Jelly-Lettuce on Raisin Bread 75
Honey Butter 99
Honey Cinnamon Toast 122
Honey-Ham-Cress AND Cranberry Sauce-Nut Meats-Lettuce on Nut Bread 76
Honey-Liederkranz Cheese AND Tomato-Lettuce on Rye ... 76
Honey Nut Filling 111
Honey-Pineapple AND Persimmon-Lettuce on Orange Biscuit 75
Honey-Raisin AND Cream Cheese-Nut Meats-Lettuce on Raisin Bread 75
Honey-Turkey AND Cream Cheese-Olive-Nut-Lettuce on Boston Brown Bread 76
Honey-Walnut Meats AND Toasted Marshmallow-Shredded Coconut on Orange Bread 75
Horseradish Butter 99

Jam Butter 99
Jelly Butter 99
Jellied Chicken AND Tomato-Lettuce on White 76
Jellied Crab Meat AND String Beans Salad-Lettuce on White 76
Jellied Lobster AND Tomato-Cress on Toast 77

Jellied Minced Ham-Apple AND Cucumber-Cole Slaw on Toasted Rye 77
Jellied Ox Tongue-Cress AND Swiss Cheese-Lettuce on Whole Wheat Bread 77
Jellied Turkey-Cress AND Bacon-Tomato-Lettuce on White 77
Jellied Veal-Cress AND Tomato-Lettuce on White 77
Jelly (any kind)-Banana AND Peanut Butter-Lettuce on Orange Bread 78
Jelly Toast Roll 122
Jocko Toast 123

Lamb Sandwich 11
Lamb Hash Sandwich 11
Lemon Butter 100
Liederkranz AND Catsup Sandwich 28
Liederkranz AND Onion Sandwich 29
Liederkranz AND Tomato Sandwich 29
Liver AND Bacon Filling ...111
Liver AND Bacon Sandwich .. 11
Liver AND Egg Filling 111
Liver AND Olive Filling ...111
Liverwurst-Bacon AND Anchovy-Tomato - Lettuce on Toasted Whole Wheat 78
Liverwurst-Bermuda Onion AND Corned Beef-Lettuce on Toasted Roll 79
Liverwurst Butter 100
Liverwurst-Cole Slaw AND American Cheese-Lettuce on Toasted Rye 78
Liverwurst - Cress AND Cream Cheese-Nut-Lettuce on Toast. 78
Liverwurst-Cucumber AND Tongue-Lettuce on Rye 79
Liverwurst-Fruit-Nut AND Ham-Tomato-Lettuce on Rye 79
Liverwurst-Pickle Relish AND Bacon-Tomato-Lettuce on Toasted Rye 78
Liverwurst - Potato Salad AND Swiss Cheese-Lettuce on Rye 79
Liverwurst-Red Cole Slaw AND Roquefort - Lettuce on Whole Wheat Bread 79
Liverwurst-Sliced Egg AND Tomato-Grated Onion-Lettuce on Rye 80
Liverwurst-Tomato AND American Cheese-Lettuce on Toasted Rye 78
Lobster Butter 100
Lobster-Catsup-Dill AND Tomato-Nut-Olive-Lettuce on Rye. 80

INDEX—(Continued)

	Page
Lobster-Chopped Cress AND Tomato-Green Pepper Rings on Whole Wheat	80
Lobster Salad-Nut Meats AND Sliced Pineapple-Lettuce on Toast	80
Lobster-Tartar Sauce AND Fried Mushrooms-Lettuce on White	80
Luncheon Toast	123
Maple Sugar Toast	123
Marmalade Almond Toast	123
Marmalade Toast	123
Melba Toast	124
Midinette Filling	111
Milk Toast I	124
Milk Toast II	124
Molasses Butter	100
Mushroom-Chicken AND Bacon-Sliced Tomato-Lettuce on Toast	81
Mushroom-Chopped Bacon AND Tomato-Lettuce on Toast	81
Mushroom - Chopped Egg AND Pineapple-Lettuce on Toasted Raisin Bread	81
Mushroom-Crab Meat AND Tuna Fish Salad-Lettuce on Toast	81
Mushroom-Fried Onion AND Tomato-Bacon-Lettuce on Toasted Rye	81
Mustard Butter	100
Nut Butter	100
Nut Meats-Chopped Liver AND Apple-Celery Salad-Lettuce on Rye	82
Nut Meats-Cranberry Jelly AND Turkey - Lettuce on Toasted French Bread	82
Nut Meats-Fig-Cress AND Veal-Dill-Lettuce on Orange Peel Bread	82
Nut Meats - Olive Meats - Green Pepper AND American Cheese on Raisin Bread	82
Nut Meats-Olive Meats-Whipped Cream AND Pineapple-Lettuce on Fig Bread	82
Olive-Pimiento Butter	100
Onion-Baked Beans AND Frankfurter-Pickle-Lettuce on Boston Brown Bread	83
Onion-Dill-Cucumber-Radish AND Ham-Lettuce on Rye	83
Onion-Nut Meats AND Liver-Bacon-Lettuce on Toast	84

	Page
Onion-Pineapple-Lettuce AND Tomato-Bacon-Lettuce on Toast	83
Onion Salad-Cucumber AND Tomato - Chopped Bacon - Lettuce on Rye	83
Orange Butter	100
Orange AND Grapefruit Marmalade, Cottage Cheese Filling	112
ORIGIN OF SANDWICHES	3
Paprika Butter	101
Parmesan Cheese AND Anchovy Sandwich	29
Parmesan Cheese AND Shrimp Sandwich	29
Parmesan Cheese AND Tomato Paste Sandwich	30
Parsley Butter	100
Peach and Nut Meats Filling	112
Peanut Butter	100
Peanut Butter-Bacon AND Tomato-Lettuce on Toasted Rye	84
Peanut Butter-Banana AND Orange Marmalade-Lettuce on Baking Powder Biscuit	87
Peanut Butter-Celery Stalks AND Tongue-Raisin-Tomato-Lettuce on Rye	86
Peanut Butter-Chopped Cress AND Cream Cheese-Celery on Honey Bread	84
Peanut Butter-Chopped Walnut AND Pot Cheese - Chives on Rye or White	85
Peanut Butter - Cranberry AND Crushed Bacon - Banana - Cress on Baking Powder Biscuit	87
Peanut Butter - Cream Cheese - Poppy Seeds AND Pineapple-Cress on Date Bread	86
Peanut Butter-Dates-Nut AND Tomato-Onion-Lettuce on Orange Bread	88
Peanut Butter-Ham and Egg Salad-Lettuce on Toasted Rye	87
Peanut Butter - Lettuce - Green Pepper AND Tongue - Swiss Cheese-Lettuce on Raisin Bread	85
Peanut Butter-Olive Meats AND American Cheese - Dill on Toasted Rye	85
Peanut Butter-Olive-Nut Meats AND Tomato-Bacon-Cress on Pumpernickel	84
Peanut Butter-Orange Marmalade AND American Cheese-Cress on Nut Bread	86

INDEX—(Continued)

Peanut Butter - Orange Marmalade AND Swiss Cheese-Cress on Date Nut Bread 85
Peanut Butter - Pimiento - Green Pepper AND Swiss Cheese-Lettuce on White 88
Peanut Butter-Pineapple AND American Cheese-Lettuce on Corn Bread 84
Peanut Butter - Pineapple AND Liederkranz-Lettuce on Orange Rye Bread 86
Peanut Butter-Prunes AND Pork-Sweet Pickle-Lettuce on Nut Bread 87
Peanut Butter-Red Cole Slaw AND Pineapple - Lettuce on Nut Bread 85
Peanut Butter-Sardine AND Potato Salad-Lettuce on Rye . 87
Peanut Butter-Sliced Orange AND Celery Green-Lettuce on Cheese Biscuit 86
Peanut Butter Toast 124
Pimiento Butter 101
Pimiento Cheese AND Deviled Ham Sandwiches 30
Pimiento Cheese AND Watercress Sandwich 30
Pineapple Cinnamon Toast ..124
Pineapple Ginger Butter 101
Pork - Apple - Cress AND String Beans Salad-Lettuce on Rye 89
Pork-Apple Sauce AND Cabbage Salad-Lettuce on Rye 88
Pork-Baked Beans AND Tomato-Lettuce on White or Rye 89
Pork - Dill - Green Pepper Rings AND American Cheese - Cress on Pumpernickel 83
Pork-Orange-Onion AND Tomato-Lettuce on Rye 89
Pork-Pineapple-Cress AND Tomato-Dill-Lettuce on Nut Bread. 89
Pork Sandwich 12
Pork-Swiss Cheese AND Potato Salad-Lettuce on Rye 88
Potted Meat Butter 101
Potted Meat Toast Egg Sauce.125
Prune Butter 101
Prunes AND Nut Filling 112

Roast Beef Sandwich 12
Roquefort Cheese Butter 101
Roquefort Cheese-Camembert AND Ham Filling 113
Roquefort Cheese AND Chicken Sandwich 30

Roquefort Cheese - Caviar - Egg AND Tomato Sandwich .. 30
Roquefort Cheese AND Cress Filling 112
Roquefort Cheese Filling 112
Roquefort Cheese AND Nut Filling.113
Roquefort Cheese AND Worcestershire Sauce Sandwich ... 31
Rum Tum Ditty 125

Salmon Butter 102
Salmon Club Sandwich 12
Salmon Salad-Cress AND Asparagus Tips-Tomato-Lettuce on Toast 89
Salmon Salad-Nut Meats AND Sliced Egg-Lettuce on Toast 90
Salmon Salad-Raw Spinach AND Tomato-Bacon-Lettuce on White 90
Salmon-Sweet Relish AND Egg-Apple-Lettuce on White or Rye 90
Salmon - Walnuts - Olives - Celery AND American Cheese-Cress on Toast 90
SANDWICH COSTS 128
SANDWICH FILLINGS 102
SANDWICH FILLING SUGGESTIONS 103
SANDWICH GARNISHINGS .. 5
SANDWICH PROFITS CHECKING CHART 126
Sardine - American Cheese AND Shrimp Salad - Lettuce on Toasted Whole Wheat 92
Sardine-Anchovy-Cress AND Bacon-Cucumber-Tomato-Cress on Rye 93
Sardine - Bacon AND Tomato - Sweet Relish-Lettuce on Rye 93
Sardine-Broiled Onion AND Swiss Cheese - Lettuce on W h o l e Wheat Bread 93
Sardine Butter 101
Sardine Club Sandwich 13
Sardine - Cress AND Caraway Cheese-Lettuce on Nut Bread 91
Sardine AND Egg Sandwich au Gratin 13
Sardine-Egg AND Scallions-Radishes-Lettuce on White or Rye 92
Sardine (mashed) -Green Pepper - Pimiento AND Salami-Lettuce on White 94
Sardine (mashed) - Horseradish AND Shrimp Salad on Rye. 94
Sardine - Lettuce AND Tomato-Anchovy-Lettuce on White . 91

INDEX—(Continued)

	Page
Sardine-Olive-Lettuce AND Tomato - Cucumber - Lettuce on White or Rye	93
Sardine-Onion-Cress AND Swiss Cheese-Dill-Lettuce on Whole Wheat	92
Sardine-Nut Meats AND Crab Meat Salad-Lettuce on Orange Bread	93
Sardine (mashed)-Nut Meats-Olive AND Salami - Tomato - Lettuce on Rye	94
Sardine (mashed)-Pineapple AND Tomato - Anchovy - Lettuce on Whole Wheat	94
Sardine-Scrambled Egg AND Tomato-Lettuce on Whole Wheat	91
Sardine-Sliced Egg AND Bermuda Onion-Pineapple-Cress on Rye	91
Sardine - Tomato AND Baked Beans-Lettuce on Whole Wheat Bread	91
Sardine - Tomato AND Cucumber-Onion-Lettuce on Rye	92
Sardine - Tomato AND Onion - Caviar-Lettuce on Rye	92
Schnitzelbank Cheese Pot Sandwiches	31
Scrambled Egg Sandwich	13
Shrimp Butter	101
Shrimp Salad - Cucumber AND Tomato-Green Pepper-Lettuce on Boston Brown Bread	95
Shrimp Salad-Nut Meats AND American Cheese-Lettuce on Rye	95
Shrimp Salad-Shredded Pineapple AND Tomato-Lettuce on Toast	94
Shrimp Salad-Tomato AND Veal-Green Pepper-Rings-Lettuce on Pumpernickel	95
Spicy American Cheese Filling	113
Spicy Ham Filling	113
Spicy Salmon Filling	115
Spicy Savory Filling	114
Spicy Sardine Filling	114
Spicy Shrimp AND Caper Mayonnaise Filling	114
Steak AND Eggplant Sandwich	13
Steak AND French Fried Onions Sandwich	14
Steak AND Fried Tomatoes Sandwich	14
Steak Sandwich	13
SUGGESTIONS FOR SEASONED AND COMPOUNDED BUTTERS FOR SANDWICHES	97

	Page
Swiss Cheese AND Asparagus Sandwich	31
Swiss Cheese AND Bacon Sandwich	32
Swiss Cheese AND Cole Slaw Sandwich	32
Swiss Cheese-Corned Beef AND Bologna Sandwich	32
Swiss Cheese AND Crabmeat Sandwich	32
Swiss Cheese AND Egg Sandwich	32
Swiss Cheese AND Ham Sandwich	33
Swiss Cheese AND Liverwurst Sandwich	33
Swiss Cheese AND Potato Salad Sandwich	33
Swiss Cheese AND Pork Sandwich	33
Swiss Cheese AND Roast Beef Sandwich	33
Swiss Cheese AND Salami Sandwich	33
Swiss Cheese AND Tongue Sandwich	34
Swiss Cheese AND Tomato Sandwich	34
Swiss Cheese AND Turkey Sandwich	34
Tarragon Butter	102
Texas Filling	115
TOASTS	116
Toasted Coconut Strips	125
Tomato French Toast Cheese Sauce	125
Tongue AND Ham Filling	115
Tongue AND Horseradish Filling	115
Tongue AND Pork Filling	116
Tomato Buns Sandwich	14
Tomato Salad-Bacon AND American Cheese-Cole Slaw-Cress on Rye	95
Tongue Sandwich	14
Turkey AND Mushroom Sauce Sandwich	14
Turkey Sandwich	14
Tuna Salad-Pimiento AND Sliced Egg-Green Pepper Rings on Rye	96
Tuna-Tomato-Dill AND Anchovy-Red Cole Slaw-Lettuce on Rye	95
Veal Cutlet Sandwich	15
Vegetable Butter	102
Vegetable Salad-Cress AND Asparagus Tips-Red Cabbage on White or Rye	96
Wall Street Sandwich	15
Water Toast	125
Welsh Rarebit Sandwich	15
Western Sandwich	15